READER'S DIGEST
RAIN FORESTS

n forest, day dawns within half an hour of 6 am
ut the year. As the Sun rises, it burns away the mist and
eveal a clear blue sky. By midday, the temperature is around
numidity is 80 per cent. This builds up to a daily storm, as the sky
ulonimbus clouds, and a bolt of lightning and crash of thunder
ownpour – rain forests did not get their name for nothing.
ists have the greatest diversity and numbers of animal species
the planet, yet an observer is hard pressed to see anything at
with their surroundings, their presence given away by the
nch, the rustle of leaves or an abrupt piercing call.

LONG-TAILED HERMIT HUMMINGBIRD Hovering in front of a heliconia blossom, this South American hummingbird uses its long bill to reach the nectaries deep within the flower. In doing so, its head gets dusted with pollen, which it carries to another flower. Some hermit hummingbird species build their nests in heliconias.

SLOTH The brown-throated, three-toed sloth hangs out in a Panama rain forest. Unlike most other mammals, the sloth has hair that hangs down from its stomach to its back, helping it to shed rain in its usual upside-down position. The sloth may be slow, but it can slash an attacker with its razor-sharp claws. During the mating season, female sloths attract males with loud, high-pitched shrieks, which sound like a shrill 'aa-ee'.

LEAFCUTTER ANTS
A line of leafcutter ants winds along a branch, each carrying a piece of leaf from the tree to their underground nest. The leaves fuel fungus gardens that the ants cultivate. These industrious insects can be pests. A colony can number more than 8 million ants and strip a fruit tree of all its leaves in 24 hours.

HOWLER MONKEYS

In the canopy of South and Central American rain forests, a chorus of howler monkeys greets the dawn. First grunts and then a cacophony of roars declare that this part of the forest is theirs during the day. The calls are so loud they can be heard more than 5 km away.

DAY

In the rai
througho
clouds to r
35°C and
darkens with huge cum
announce a torrential d
Tropical rain fore
of any environment on
all. Most animals blend
movement of a bra

FIJI CRESTED IGUANA

A metre-long crested iguana warms up under the rising Sun. One of two iguana species in the rain forests of Fiji and other South Pacific islands, it eats leaves, shoots, fruits and flowers, especially sweet hibiscus.

TENT-MAKING BATS

A group of tiny tent-making bats makes a daytime roost on the underside of a large banana leaf, bent to form a protective envelope, in the forests of South and Central America. Each group consists of a male with his harem of females. The male will defend his tent and his harem against any intruders or challengers.

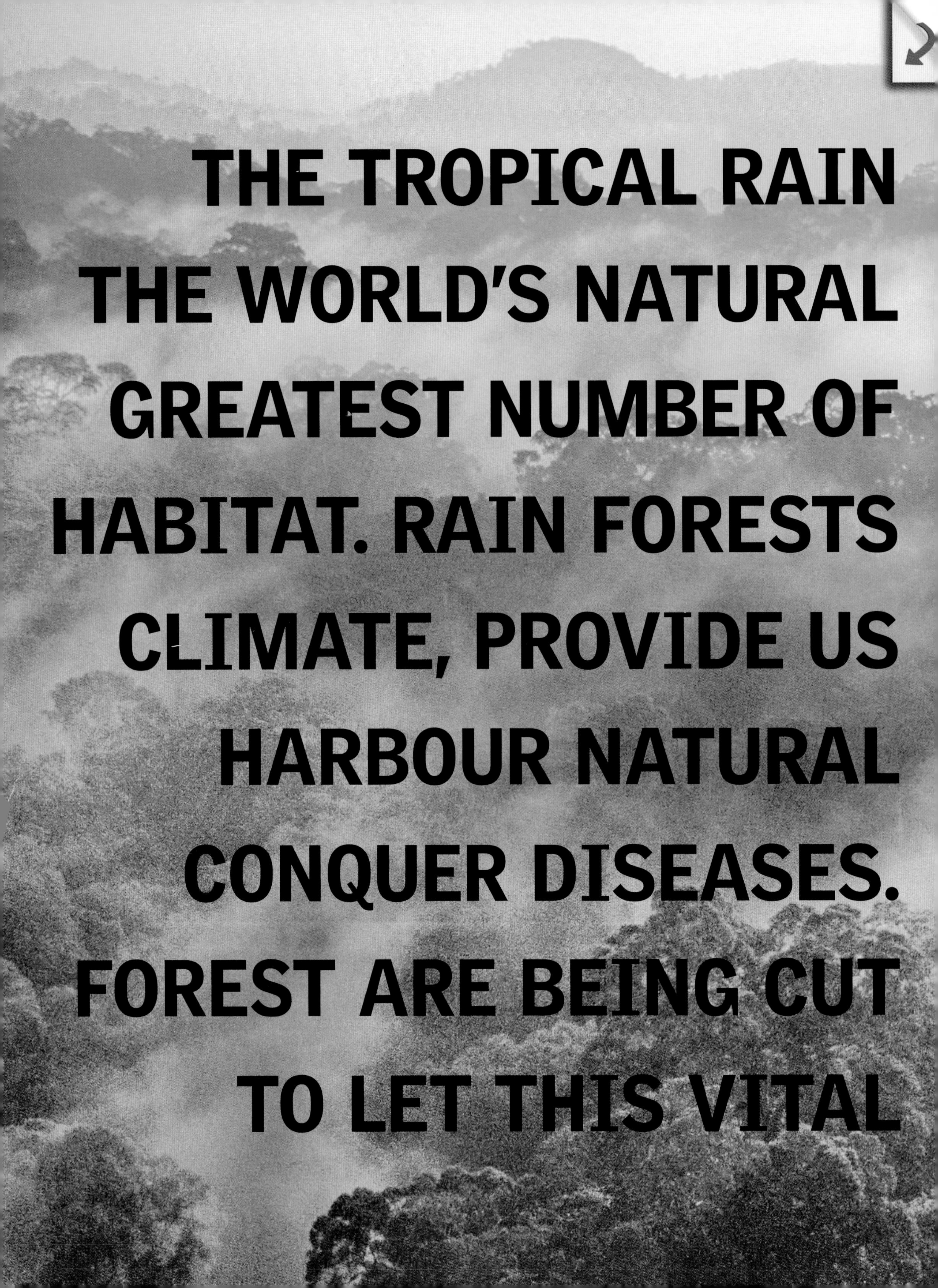

THE TROPICAL RAIN
THE WORLD'S NATURAL
GREATEST NUMBER OF
HABITAT. RAIN FORESTS
CLIMATE, PROVIDE US
HARBOUR NATURAL
CONQUER DISEASES.
FOREST ARE BEING CUT
TO LET THIS VITAL

FORESTS ARE ONE OF WONDERS, HOME TO THE SPECIES OF ANY KNOWN HELP TO CONTROL WITH FOODS AND CHEMICALS THAT MAY YET VAST SWATHES OF DOWN. CAN WE AFFORD RESOURCE DISAPPEAR?

NIGHT

At dusk, the skies over the rain forest clear. Sunset comes abruptly and within half an hour of 6 pm each day. It is marked by clouds of mosquitoes that appear in the still air between the ground and the canopy. There is scarcely any change in temperature between night and day. Tree frogs set up a rhythmic, monotonous chorus from the branches of the canopy, and bats swoop through the warm night air. On the forest floor, cats and nocturnal foragers rustle in the undergrowth, seeking prey or fruit to feast on.

LONG-TONGUED BAT

An especially noisy, fast-flying bat from Central and South America, the long-tongued bat owes its name to an unusually long, narrow, extensible tongue. This has brush-like papillae (projections) at the tip to lap up nectar from night-opening flowers.

TREE FROG

In the swamp rain forest of Costa Rica, a male golden palm tree frog inflates its throat as it calls from the forest floor. The frog spends most of its life high in the canopy but comes down during the breeding season. Here, it is exposed to dangers from snakes, frog-eating spiders and fishing bats.

OCELOT

This small, spotted cat is almost invisible when out hunting by night. It pursues its prey at all levels in the forest, catching monkeys, rodents, reptiles, fish, amphibians and birds. The ocelot is strongly territorial and will fight an intruder sometimes to the death. It is most common in South and Central America, but has been spotted as far north as Texas.

HAWK MOTH

As daylight fades, an *Erinnyis* sphinx hawk moth takes to the wing in a Venezuelan forest. Males find females by scent. Eggs are laid on the leaves of papaya, guava, poinsettia and saffron plum, which also provide food for hawk moth caterpillars. Adult hawk moths are nectar-feeders, with a remarkable ability to fly far and fast and to hover – like a hawk – as they sip nectar from flowers.

NIGHT MONKEY

Big, brown, owl-like eyes are a sign of the nocturnal way of life that gives the night monkey of South and Central America its name – it is the only true monkey that is active at night. Unlike most other monkeys, the night monkey does not have colour vision, but it has superb spatial resolution at low light levels.

KINKAJOU
A relative of the raccoon, the kinkajou of South and Central America is a fruit-eater. It also uses its tongue to lick nectar from flowers – a habit that has earned it the nickname of 'honey bear'. A fully prehensile tail helps it to hang from branches, leaving its forepaws free to pick fruit. Kinkajous forage alone by night. During the day, they sleep together in family groups.

WHITE-NOSED COATI
Another relative of the raccoon, the coati of the New World rain forests eats just about anything it can find, including fruit and insects. In places where humans hunt the coati for the pot, it is nocturnal. The coati is equally at home on the forest floor as in the trees, where it uses its tail to balance.

RAIN FORESTS

1 FORESTS OF RAIN

16 BETWEEN THE TROPICS
21 MADAGASCAR
24 WALLACEA
26 RAIN-FOREST CLIMATE
28 WET AND DRY
30 THE RAIN-FOREST POWERHOUSE
36 TIMBER, FOOD AND MEDICINES
38 TEMPERATE RAIN FORESTS

2 THE BATTLE FOR LIGH

44 FOREST LEVELS
46 FOREST FLOOR
48 UNDERSTOREY
52 CANOPY
58 OVERSTOREY
60 RAIN-FOREST CAVES

5 FOREST PREDATORS

110 AERIAL PREDATORS
112 TERRESTRIAL PREDATORS
116 PREDATORY ANTS
118 INSECT-EATING SPECIALISTS
120 RAIN-FOREST SPIDERS
122 MEALS OF BLOOD

6 LIVING TOGETHER

126 COLONIES
130 STRANGE PARTNERSHIPS
134 POOLS IN THE SKY

DISAPPEARING FORESTS

Tropical forests are disappearing at an alarming rate. This table, based on statistics from the UN's Food and Agricultural Organisation, shows how much forest was lost in the following countries between 1990 and 2005 and the extent of remaining forest cover (as a percentage of each country's total land area) in 2005.

COUNTRY	FOREST LOSS (hectares)	FOREST LOSS (percentage)	REMAINING COVER IN 2005 (percentage)
Brazil	2 821 933	8.1	57.2
Indonesia	1 871 467	24.1	48.8
Democratic Republic of Congo	461 400	4.9	58.9
Nigeria	409 667	35.7	12.2
Venezuela	287 533	8.3	54.1
Bolivia	270 333	6.5	54.2
Philippines	227 467	32.3	24.0
Cameroon	220 000	13.4	45.6
Ecuador	197 600	21.5	39.2
Honduras	182 467	37.1	41.5
Cambodia	166 600	19.3	59.2
Papua New Guinea	139 067	6.6	65.0

INTRODUCTION

TROPICAL RAIN FORESTS TEEM WITH LIFE. They cover about 6 per cent of the Earth's land surface, yet account for 50 per cent of its biodiversity. Colourful birds and butterflies flit through the sunlit canopy and troops of chattering monkeys swing from tree to tree gathering fruits, flowers or handfuls of leaves. Snakes and tree frogs sit motionless on gnarled branches, waiting to pluck their prey from the air, while down on the forest floor rats and small pigs snuffle amongst the leaf litter. Sleek, nimble cats glide through the foliage like ghosts in the gloom. Beard-like lichens, delicate ferns, gaudy bromeliads and exquisite orchids festoon the trees, while vines and lianas drape them in long, straggling strands.

Yet for all this bustle of life, a visitor to the rain forest would often be hard pressed to see any creatures there at all. For most of the time, the animals of the rain forest are beautifully camouflaged, blending in with their background. **Activity** usually increases at **dawn and dusk**, and frogs and insects can be incredibly noisy at night, but during the best part of the day the rain forest is **largely silent**. Nor is it the dense jungle so often depicted in feature films. Walking in a rain forest is not much different from walking in a European

forest. There is **little undergrowth**, apart from mosses, ferns and other small plants, to impede progress. Only at the forest edge or in clearings, where **light** can penetrate to the floor, is the tangle of vegetation impenetrable.

Rain forests are remarkably **young**. By examining fossils in rocks from millions of years ago, scientists have worked out that the **first tropical rain forests** appeared 60–100 millions years ago. Many of today's forests grew up after the end of the last Ice Age, which started its decline about 15 000 years ago, and some may be no more 2000 years old. Concealed in these forests are some of the **keys to our future**. Not only are the rain forests the 'lungs of the Earth', which help to **control its climate**, but still hidden in their depths may lie the natural chemicals we need to **beat disease**. Yet this precious resource is under threat. Many rain-forest species have yet to be discovered, but because of **deforestation** many may be extinct before we know they are there at all. Trees are being cut down at a rate of **2000 a minute**, and only one is replanted for every 10 cut down. It is thought that 50 species are disappearing each day. With only 5 per cent of the world's tropical forests currently protected in national parks or nature reserves, all the tropical rain forest may be gone within 200 years.

FORESTS
OF RAIN

UPWARDS OF 5 MILLION SPECIES OF PLANTS, ANIMALS, FUNGI AND BACTERIA – nearly half of all life on Earth, according to some estimates – thrive in tropical rain forests. Conditions in rain forests, such as this one in French Guiana, are perfect for life to proliferate. A warm year-round climate, with a stable air temperature between 22°C and 34°C, and enormous quantities of rain – up to 10 920 mm annually – provide ideal growing conditions for dense vegetation. This in turn provides food and shelter for an extraordinary number of animals. The dominant plants are trees, and much of rain-forest life resides in their tightly packed canopy. Down below, a variety of shade-tolerant plants grow in the gloom of the forest floor. Most of the nutrients in a rain forest are found not in the soil, but locked up in the trees themselves.

BETWEEN THE TROPICS

THE WORLD'S MOST EXTENSIVE RAIN FORESTS ARE TROPICAL, spreading across large swathes of South and Central America, Africa and South-east Asia between the Tropics of Cancer and Capricorn. Tropical rain forests once covered 12 per cent of the Earth's land surface. Today, the figure is less than 6 per cent, as people cut down trees for timber or to use the land for farming. Nearly half of the surviving tropical rain forests are in South and Central America. A little under 30 per cent are in Africa, 16 per cent in Asia and 9 per cent in Australia. All are under threat and steadily disappearing.

Basin of diversity

By far the largest tract of unbroken rain forest covers the basin of the River Amazon, which with its 1100 major tributaries drains nearly 40 per cent of South America's land surface. Here, a vast mosaic of rain forest mingled with seasonal and flooded forests covers 8.2 million km^2, encompassing much of Brazil along with parts of eastern Bolivia, Peru, Ecuador and Colombia.

During the last Ice Age, the Amazon region was probably savannah and mountain forest, among which only a few pockets of rain forest survived. In each of these rain-forest 'islands', populations of animals were isolated and new species evolved. By the time the vast Amazonian rain forest reformed after the Ice Age, species had diversified massively, giving the extraordinary range of different creatures we recognise today.

Apart from the Amazonian forest, South America has other substantial tracts of rain forest, bordering the Orinoco River as it flows through Colombia and Venezuela and along the continent's north-eastern coast from Guyana, through Surinam to French Guiana. In Central America, rain forests survive in Panama, Costa Rica, Belize, Guatemala, Honduras, Nicaragua

CENTRAL AMERICA

AMAZON RIVER
BASIN

FOREST BEAUTY An orchid clings to the vertical trunk of a tree in Central America. The site on the side of the tree looks precarious, but it contains an entire garden in miniature, complete with soil and even earthworms.

and Mexico, although 30 per cent of these have been cut down in recent years. Rain forests once clothed many of the Caribbean islands, but few survive today, mainly on islands in the eastern Caribbean, such as Trinidad, Dominica and St Lucia.

Africa's disappearing forests

In Africa, 2 million km² of rain forest in the Congo River Basin and in neighbouring Cameroon represent the world's second largest tract of rain forest, covering about 7 per cent of Africa's land surface. At one time there was much more, with unbroken forest stretching from Senegal on the west coast to the walls of the Great Rift Valley in the south-east. One of the most easterly remnants of this vast tree cover is Kenya's Kakamega Forest. In West Africa, more than 80 per cent of the original forest has gone – in the quarter century since 1980, deforestation rates in Africa have been higher than in any of the world's other rain-forest regions.

Six nations – the Republic of Congo, the Democratic Republic of Congo, Cameroon, the Central African Republic, Gabon and Equatorial Guinea – are custodians of the surviving tracts of African rain forest, but these may not last much longer, due more to global warming than human logging. Africa's rain-forest region was savannah during the last Ice Age, and it could well return to grassland as a result of climate change.

Africa's rain forests are not thought to be as rich in species as their South American or Asian counterparts, but with large parts of

DEMOCRATIC REPUBLIC OF CONGO

GATHERING FOOD A lowland gorilla forages for mineral-rich water plants in a bais, *a swamp clearing in the Congo Basin rain forest. The clearing is also an important place for gorilla groups to meet.*

FOREST AND WATER Ecuador's dramatic San Rafael Falls (overleaf), where the Coca River, filled with meltwater from the Andes, plunges down into the Amazonian rain forest.

TROPIC OF CANCER

CONGO RIVER BASIN

EQUATOR

SOUTH-EAST ASIAN RAIN FORESTS

TROPIC OF CAPRICORN

BORNEO

TROPICAL ZONE Circling the globe 23.5 degrees north and south of the Equator, the Tropics of Cancer and Capricorn bound the zone where the world's largest rain forests grow. Right: Lowland rain forest in the Danum Valley of Sabah, a Malaysian state in northern Borneo.

3 ANIMAL POWER

64 HANGING BY A TAIL
66 UNEXPECTED AVIATORS
68 FOREST OF THE APES
72 SIGNALLING
76 EXTRAVAGANT BIRDS
80 COLOUR CHANGE

4 FOOD FOR ALL

84 NECTAR FEEDERS
86 KINGDOMS OF MONKEYS
90 FRUIT AND NUT CASES
96 RAIN-FOREST DWARFS
100 LARGE HERBIVORES
102 LEAF-EATERS
104 DIETARY SUPPLEMENTS
106 RAIN-FOREST GIANTS

7 WATER WORLDS

138 RAIN-FOREST RIVERS
140 FLOODED FOREST
146 SEA IN A RIVER
148 FRESHWATER GIANTS
150 FOREST FROGS
152 FUTURE OF RAIN FORESTS

FLOWING FORESTS Rain-forest trees grow right down to the shoreline of a slow-moving tributary of the Orinoco in Venezuela.

Africa taken up by deserts and scrub, they still contain more than half of all plant and animal species on the continent. They are also home to our nearest relatives – bonobos, chimpanzees and gorillas.

Riches in Asia and Australia

The diversity of Asia's rain forests is second only to those of South America. In a single 100 m^2 plot of Malaysian rain forest, scientists counted 780 species of tree – more than the total number of tree species in the whole of Europe.

Rain forests grow throughout Indonesia and Malaysia, in South-east Asia and on the Indian subcontinent. Like rain forests everywhere, these are fast disappearing. On the Indonesian island of Sulawesi, 80 per cent of its rain forests have been destroyed in recent decades. The only forests that remain grow on mountain slopes higher than 1500 m above sea level, yet these are home to an extraordinary range of rare species – half of the mammal species (100 per cent if bats are excluded) and a third of the bird species there are found nowhere else in the world.

Australia has two small areas of unprotected tropical rain forest, mostly along the coastal plains and in the mountain areas of the Cape York Peninsula, Queensland. The island continent's forests may be small, but they are a wildlife hotspot, harbouring a third of Australia's marsupials and amphibian species and two-thirds of its butterflies. At one time, when sea levels were lower than today, Australia's rain forests were linked by a land bridge to those in New Guinea, so the two regions share many of the same plants and animal species. It is thought that Queensland's rain forests are larger today than they were at the end of the Ice Age, but the danger now is that they may disappear, because up to a third of the area is threatened by human development.

The South Pacific's misty forests

Many of the higher islands in the southern Pacific Ocean have pockets of mist-enshrouded rain forest. In the Solomon Islands, forests in the interior of the main island have a rich flora, including more than 4500 species, 123 of which have identifiable medical properties. On the uninhabited island of Tetepare, there are swathes of pristine rain forest. They are among the world's few areas of rain forest still untouched by the commercial loggers.

The Cook Islands have remnants of rain forests, too. On the popular holiday island of Rarotonga, the upper slopes of its central volcano have some of the best remaining tracts of primary rain forest in eastern Polynesia. They are home to four bird species found nowhere else in the world – the Rarotonga starling, the Mangaia kingfisher, the Rarotonga monarch and the Atiu swiftlet, an unusual cave-nesting species.

MADAGASCAR

PIERCING CALLS GREET THE DAWN ON A NOVEMBER MORNING IN MADAGASCAR'S EASTERN RAIN FORESTS – so loud that they echo through the entire forest. The animals responsible for this extraordinary sound are large, black and white, panda-like creatures called indris. They are members of the island's most striking animal group, the lemurs – primitive primates, related to bush babies and lorises, which occupy the place in Madagascar's forests filled by monkeys elsewhere.

Indris also have a special place in Malagasy legend, which tells how two brothers went their separate ways. One turned to farming to become the first human; the other went to the forest to become the first indri. The indri now makes his melancholy cry in mourning for his lost brother. The calls involve all the members of an indri group, including any youngsters in the family. At first, they roar a prelude, followed by a three-minute high-pitched duet by the dominant adult pair. Each burst of sound lasts for about five seconds, and as the call progresses, the pitch gradually drops. It is probably the most haunting sound from a rain forest anywhere on Earth.

The world's fourth-largest island, Madagascar lies in the Indian Ocean off Africa's east coast and is home to a wealth of animal and plant life found nowhere else on Earth. Its rain forests are restricted to a narrow corridor, running north-south along the eastern half of the island, and they are being cut down fast. Even so, 100 000 km^2 remain, the repository of an estimated 10 000 plant species, 80 per cent of which are unique to Madagascar. Its animals are equally unusual. Aside from bats, which can fly across the sea, all Madagascar's mammals are endemic, meaning they are found only there and on some surrounding islands. There are no big cats – their place as top predators is taken by civet and mongoose-like predators, such as the fossa, fanalouc, fanaloka and striped civet.

Living laboratory

When the super-continent of Gondwana split up about 165 million years ago, Madagascar and India separated from Africa. Then, about 88 million years ago, the two landmasses parted company, with India continuing on its way towards Asia. The Mozambique Channel, which now separates Madagascar from

NIGHT-FEEDER The aye-aye may look bizarre but its bulbous eyes and large ears are perfectly adapted for a nocturnal lifestyle.

FOSSA

THE TOP PREDATOR

IN MADAGASCAR'S RAIN FORESTS IS THE FOSSA. This agile and ferocious cat-like member of the civet-mongoose family is the island's largest carnivorous mammal. Adult males are 70–80 cm long and weigh 6–10 kg – about twice the size of a domestic cat. Females tend to be slightly smaller. Both are voracious hunters, taking fish, birds and lemurs.

The fossa (pronounced 'foosa') is rarely seen and was once thought to be strictly nocturnal, but recent studies reveal that it is active both day and night, sometimes travelling 20 km or more when hunting for prey. It leaps from tree to tree like a squirrel, using its 90 cm tail for balance. Fiercely defensive of its territory, it is a perfect killing machine. When seizing prey, a fossa can put on an explosive burst of speed as it grabs, then crushes a lemur's head in its powerful jaws, and slashes at the creature's belly with sharp claws. Local Malagasy mythology abounds with stories – many of them greatly exaggerated – of how dangerous the fossa is. In some, it is said to have taken cattle and even attacked people. Naughty children are told that if they are not good, the fossa will come and take them away. Its flatulence alone is reported to have killed a coop of chickens.

The fossa is found in the wild only in Madagascar, and there are thought to be no more that 2500 surviving individuals in the island's fragmented forests. It is considered endangered by the International Union for the Conservation of Nature and Natural Resources (IUCN); 55 are kept in captivity worldwide, 13 of them in natural enclosures at Duisburg Zoo in Germany.

VITAL STATISTICS

CLASS: Mammalia
ORDER: Carnivore
SPECIES: *Cryptoprocta ferox*
HABITAT: Rain forest
DISTRIBUTION: Madagascar
KEY FEATURES: Largest mammalian predator in Madagascar, specially adapted for hunting in trees as well as on the ground.

the African mainland, is only 400 km wide, but so deep that land bridges did not exist even in periods of lower sea levels. This means that all of the island's plants and animals – apart from occasional creatures that have flown, swum, drifted or rafted from mainland Africa – evolved there in almost complete isolation. The result is like a living evolutionary laboratory.

For medical researchers, Madagascar's plants are particularly important. On the Masoala Peninsula, one of the island's surviving rain-forest strongholds, 229 plants have tested positively as sources of anti-malarial drugs. The bark of the flowering plant *Strychnopsis thouarsii* has been shown to be especially useful against the primary liver stage of the malaria parasite. It was in Madagascar's rain forests that an effective drug against childhood leukaemia was found.

Primate survivors

Madagascar's isolation explains the dominance of the lemurs. They first appeared in the fossil record about 60 million years ago, and some grew to the size of gorillas. At that time, they existed in Africa as well as Madagascar. Then, about 20 million years ago, monkeys evolved. By that stage, the distance between the African mainland and Madgascar was too great for the monkeys to invade the island. On the mainland, the more intelligent monkeys ousted the lemurs, but lemurs survived on Madagascar. Today, they are in danger again, from the most intelligent primate of all – humans.

The largest lemurs are the indri and the diademed sifaka, two species that move through the trees with their bodies in an upright posture. They feed on fruits and leaves and rarely come to the ground, preferring to leap up to 10 m between trees. The most recently discovered lemur is the golden bamboo lemur. It feeds mainly on the shoots, leaf bases and pith of the giant bamboo, each laced with high concentrations of cyanide. It is said that the golden bamboo lemur consumes enough cyanide each day to kill a human. How it deals with the poison remains a mystery.

Perhaps the most curious inhabitant of Madagascar's forests is another lemur and the world's largest nocturnal primate – the aye-aye. It resembles a creature from the film *Gremlins*, with big eyes and ears, rodent-like teeth and an extended middle finger that probes deep into crevices for wood-boring grubs. To find the grubs, the aye-aye uses echolocation – tapping on a log or branch and listening for returning echoes. It fills the ecological niche normally occupied by a bird, the woodpecker, elsewhere in the world.

ARBOREAL PRIMATE With no monkeys to contend with, lemurs such as the diademed sifaka have thrived in Madagascar's rain forests. The sifaka eats a wide variety of plants – up to 25 different species a day.

SANDWICHED BETWEEN ASIA AND AUSTRALASIA, THE VOLCANIC ISLANDS SCIENTISTS CALL WALLACEA ARE A 'MIXING ZONE', where the plant and animal life of both continents blend. Part of Indonesia, they lie dotted across the stretch of ocean separating Java and New Guinea and are named after Alfred Russel Wallace, a British evolutionary biologist, who made a study of their flora and fauna in the 19th century.

The islands' geographical position makes them particularly fascinating to biologists, who have even created an imaginary line, the Wallace Line, running through the Malay Archipelago. The line passes between Borneo and Sulawesi in the north of the region and between Bali and Lombok in the south, and it is marked by a deep ocean channel. The plants and animals on the islands to the west of the line are of mainly Asian origin, although they also include some Australasian species. To the east of the

The geographical position of the islands makes them fascinating to biologists, who have created an imaginary line, the Wallace Line, through the Malay Archipelago.

WALLACEA

line, the situation is reversed – most plants and animals are of Australasian origin, but some are Asian. The distance between Bali and Lombok is no more than 35 km, yet many birds will not cross the open water. It has been this way for 50 million years, since the last time that Asia and Australasia were joined by a land bridge.

Split between two continents

All the islands were once densely forested, but in recent times many lowland forests have been cut down to make way for plantations and farms. The largest island is Sulawesi (once known as Celebes), which lies to the east of the Wallace Line. Its surviving rain forests are home to a number of species of Australasian origin, including

MONSTER LIZARD The water monitor is equally at home on land or in the water. Its forked tongue 'tastes' the air for signs of food. It can move faster than we can, and it runs down prey rather than setting an ambush.

MOUND BUILDER The maleo bird is found in the wild only in Sulawesi's rain forests. The female lays unusually large eggs – about five times the size of domestic chicken's eggs – in nests in the ground.

LITTLE TUSKER The male babirusa ('pig deer' in Malay) has two sets of tusks, the upper set pushing through the top of the snout. It keeps the lower tusks sharp by rubbing them against tree trunks.

the maleo, a medium-sized, chicken-like bird with large feet. It spends most of its time on the ground in dense jungle but seeks out open sandy areas to lay its eggs. Unlike most birds, it does not incubate its eggs with its own body heat, but buries them and relies on the Sun or volcanic heat to keep them warm. After two or three months, the young birds hatch out and dig their way to the surface, which may take two days. They are self-sufficient from the moment they emerge, but they must be wary of their main predators, such as pythons, pigs, cats and monitor lizards.

Sulawesi's forests also have animals of Asian origin, including two species of rare dwarf buffalo, called the lowland and mountain anoas; an endangered palm civet; seven species of macaque monkeys; and five species of tarsiers. The last group are primitive primates, related to bush babies, which come out mainly at night. They have huge goggle-like eyes and long feet, and they catch insects by jumping at them. When leaping from tree to tree, tarsiers have been known to catch birds on the wing.

Land of bizarre pigs

Of the smaller islands, Buru has kept two large blocks of upland rain forest, dominated by dipterocarps, unusual trees which produce two-winged fruit. Hiding among their boughs are at least ten rare species of bird, including the Moluccan scrub fowl, the blue-fronted lorikeet and the rufous-throated white-eye. Three species of flying fox are found in this region and nowhere else. Buru is also home to the golden or hairy babirusa, an unusual member of the pig family. The males have very distinctive curled tusks, formed from elongated upper and lower canine teeth. The upper canines grow out through the top of the snout and curl back towards the forehead. Its bizarre appearance has inspired some Indonesian ethnic groups to model their demonic masks on the babirusa's face.

Other inhabitants of the islands include a wealth of monitor lizards – each island or island group has its own species or sub-species. The largest is the Komodo dragon, the world's largest lizard, but this lives on islands with a more arid climate. A close second in size is the water monitor lizard, which lives in the islands' tropical rain forests. It grows to an imposing 3 m in length and is fast and very aggressive, using both its powerful jaws and tail when cornered. It feeds on small mammals, birds and fish, and is a good swimmer.

RAIN-FOREST CLLIMATE

AS OFTEN AS NOT, MORNING IN THE RAIN FOREST STARTS WITH A BRIGHT BLUE SKY. But as the day progresses things change dramatically. By lunchtime, the clouds are forming and the air is sticky, and by mid-afternoon the rain falls suddenly out of a densely clouded sky. It is not the light rain familiar to people living in temperate climes, but a deluge. Lightning forks to the ground accompanied by ear-shattering claps of thunder, and this happens without fail for large parts of the year.

While most places in the world measure their rainfall in millimetres, tropical rain forests have metres of rain. In the rain forests, it rains on at least 130 days each year, and in some places, such as the Amazon Basin, rain can fall on more than 250 days a year. Even so, there can be fluctuations. In some forests, rainfall is seasonal, giving wet

HEAVY RAINS Thick rainclouds hang over the forested banks of the Amazon River. The Amazon Basin is always hot and humid, and localised rainstorms can occur at any time of the year both in the 'rainy' and 'rainier' seasons. High rainfall means higher levels of fruit production and so more animal activity.

and dry seasons. It can also vary considerably from one part of a forest to another, depending on the topography and the density of trees. The air temperature, meanwhile, is consistently warm, often hot, with highs of 31°C and night-time lows rarely less than 22°C.

Weather machines

Rain forests the size of the Amazonian one have their own microclimate. About half the rainfall comes from water recycled by 'evapotranspiration' from the leaves of the rain forest's great ocean of trees – the Amazon straddles the Equator, so the Sun is overhead and its intensity is such that it evaporates huge quantities of water.

The rest of the rainfall arrives from elsewhere. In the Amazon, the trade winds bring in moisture from the Atlantic Ocean. The damp air is funnelled into the Amazon Basin, bordered by the Guiana Highlands to the north, the Andes to the west and the Brazilian Highlands to the south. Eventually, the warm, moist air is forced upwards by the mountains. In the west, it cools, condenses and precipitates as rain in the Andean foothills and as snow on the highest Andean peaks.

This substantially self-watering system affects both the climate of the Amazon region and the world climate. The region is part of the Intertropical Convergence Zone, where two major air masses meet – one from the Northern Hemisphere and the other from the Southern Hemisphere. The energy released

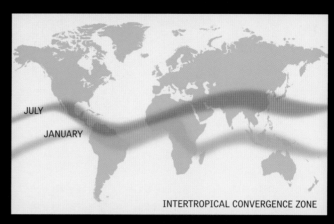

JULY

JANUARY

INTERTROPICAL CONVERGENCE ZONE

DOLDRUMS The Intertropical Convergence Zone (ITCZ), traditionally known to sailors as the Doldrums, is a belt of low pressure produced by rising, warm, moist air on either side of the Equator. It is part of the Earth's heat and moisture distribution system, and its position varies throughout the year – shown here in July (red) and January (blue).

during tropical rainstorms in this zone is immense, and it is thought to help to drive atmospheric circulation on the entire planet. In addition, vegetation in tropical rain forests absorbs heat, which helps to cool the atmosphere, as well as absorbing and retaining water. This makes large areas of tropical rain forest, such as those of the Amazon and Congo Basins, important as world climate regulators.

WET AND DRY

EVEN TROPICAL RAIN FORESTS HAVE SEASONS – TIMES WHEN THE WEATHER IS WETTER AND TIMES WHEN IT IS DRIER. There is very little variation in daylength and temperature throughout the year, but rainfall, although high overall, varies. In the Amazon Basin, for example, there is a drier season from August until November and the wettest months are from January to April. Farther north, in the rain forests of Belize in Central America, the rainy season starts modestly in June and in earnest in July. It lasts until December, followed by a relatively dry period from mid-February to May. Generally speaking, when it is dry in the rain forests to the north of the Equator, it is wet in those to the south.

This variation throughout the year affects rain-forest plants and animals. Most trees produce their flowers in the dry season when air-borne pollen is carried for longer on the drier winds. The drier conditions also mean that insects can take to the wing more easily, which helps any insect-pollinated plants. After seeds are dispersed, the saplings sprout at the onset of the rainy season. Where large trees have fallen, enabling light to reach the forest floor, the young 'pioneering' plants put on a burst of growth through the resulting gaps in the canopy. Trees that have grown up to the canopy then grow faster in the dry season, when the skies are blue for longer and more sunlight is available to support photosynthesis. The leaves are now like tiny chemical factories, industriously turning sunlight, water and carbon dioxide into sugars and starches. More than half of all rain-forest plants follow this pattern.

'Autumn' colours with new growth

With little variation in temperature and no frost to contend with, most rain-forest trees are evergreens. They do not shed their leaves seasonally, although they tend to grow new ones at the start of the wet season. New leaves are less protected by the plant's chemical defence systems and so are more vulnerable to

TREE ANTEATER The tamandua is a tree-living anteater from the Amazon. It has strong claws and a prehensile tail, together with a long nose, jaws and tongue – but no teeth. It breaks into the nests of arboreal ants and termites, favouring one more than the other at certain times of the year.

leaf-eaters, such as howler monkeys in South America and proboscis monkeys in South-east Asia. By synchronising new growth, the trees ensure that at least some of their new leaves survive, since the browsers cannot eat them all.

There is, however, a reversal of the seasonal colours seen in the rest of the world. In rain forests, the reds, yellows and oranges we normally associate with autumn appear when their trees grow new leaves. In the Australian rain forests, for example, new leaves on trees such as the Francis' water gum and riberry produce a red pigment, called anthocyanin, which protects the developing photosynthetic system in their tissues. Anthocyanin reflects red light and absorbs light at the blue end of the spectrum, so it acts like a sunscreen, preventing light from penetrating the leaf until it is ready to photosynthesise.

The variations between the wet and dry seasons affect the behaviour of animals as well. In Madagascar, sifakas reduce their foraging range and introduce an afternoon siesta during the dry season, when quality plant food is less easy to find. In French Guiana, red howler monkeys not only change their diet but also their method of locomotion. In the dry season, the howler monkeys travel on all fours along large branches through the canopy, stopping from time to time to eat leaves. In the wet season, they sit and feed on fruits – this type of food requires more concentration and manipulation.

In Brazil's Atlantic coast forest, the black lion tamarin, a small New World monkey, focuses during the wet season on fruit, which requires little travelling. In the dry season, it catches more animal food, such as crickets and grasshoppers, and forages more widely to find it. On Sulawesi in Indonesia, the spectral tarsier forages more widely during the dry season when insects are less abundant. It also shifts its diet subtly, adding beetles and bees to its wet-season feast of moths and grasshoppers.

RED FOR GO In rain forests, 'autumn colours' come with new growth, rather than old. Young leaves lack chlorophyll and so appear red.

RAIN-FOREST POWERHOUSE

THE TROPICAL RAIN FOREST IS CONTINUALLY MANUFACTURING FOOD, RECYCLING WASTE AND PRODUCING AND ABSORBING GASES. At the centre of the process is carbon, the element that forms the basis of the chemistry of life on our planet. In combination with other elements, carbon forms hydrocarbons, the main fuels of the planet; amino acids and proteins, the building blocks of life; and DNA and RNA, the blueprints for all life on Earth.

When linked to oxygen, carbon forms carbon dioxide. As one of the greenhouse gases, carbon dioxide is associated with global warming, but it is also essential to life on Earth because of photosynthesis – the process by which plants use energy from the Sun to convert water and carbon dioxide into sugars, starches and oxygen. Through photosynthesis, the most important chemical reaction in nature, carbon dioxide becomes the principal source of plant growth and so the ultimate source of food for almost all living things.

Lungs of the planet

Through photosynthesis, the rain forests play a key part in maintaining the global balance of carbon dioxide and oxygen in the atmosphere, which is why they are sometimes called the 'lungs of the planet'. By day, photosynthesising plants take in carbon dioxide and release oxygen; at night, they stop photosynthesising and switch to respiration,

THE CARBON EQUATION Carbon is exchanged constantly between plants and animals, the oceans, the atmosphere and the ground. Through photosynthesis, plants take in carbon dioxide (CO_2) from the atmosphere and produce carbon-based sugars and starches. Decaying plant materials can then be compressed and turned into coal or oil. When this is burned – in car engines or factories, for example – the carbon is released back into the atmosphere as carbon dioxide. Further carbon dioxide is given off in animal and plant respiration. In the oceans, micro-organisms called phytoplankton are also photosynthetic. They lock up carbon in their shells and when they die sink to the sea floor, eventually becoming limestone rock. This store of carbon can return to the atmosphere as carbon dioxide from volcanoes.

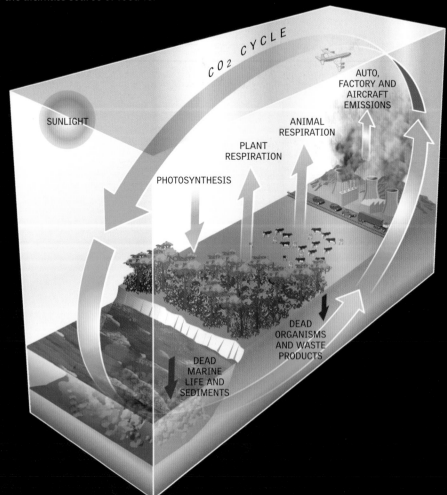

CO2 CYCLE

SUNLIGHT

AUTO, FACTORY AND AIRCRAFT EMISSIONS

ANIMAL RESPIRATION

PLANT RESPIRATION

PHOTOSYNTHESIS

DEAD ORGANISMS AND WASTE PRODUCTS

DEAD MARINE LIFE AND SEDIMENTS

so oxygen is taken in and carbon dioxide given off. Rain-forest trees are vital in the process, simply because there are so many of them.

Rain forests also store carbon. The sugars produced by photosynthesis contain carbon and so lock up carbon in plants until the plants die – a forest of trees thus acts as a huge carbon 'reservoir'. When vegetation dies and decays, the carbon in its tissues finds its way back into the atmosphere as carbon dioxide or methane. This process is accelerated when trees are felled and a forest is burned.

Faster growth

Recently, some scientists have queried whether large rain forests are carbon reservoirs, as claimed by accepted scientific wisdom, or are actually pumping out more carbon in the form of carbon dioxide than they are storing. Given the threat of global warming, the question is an important one.

Currently, human activity pumps an estimated 6 billion tonnes of carbon dioxide into the atmosphere each year, mainly through the burning of wood and fossil fuels, but scientists can only find and measure 3 billion. The other 3 billion tonnes goes somewhere else, and scientists have recently discovered where. During the past few decades, the trees of the Amazonian rain forest have been growing more rapidly than they used to. This is because they have been actively absorbing the extra carbon dioxide from the atmosphere and so locking up the carbon. In this way, the rain forests clearly act as a carbon reservoir, helping to slow global warming.

Even so, the rain forests cannot be considered a long-term solution to the problem of global warming. If temperatures carry on rising, some rain forests will dry out. With a greater risk of fire, any carbon they were storing would be released into the atmosphere, resulting in further warming. We need to protect the forests, because they help to offset the effects of raised levels of atmospheric carbon dioxide. If they were eradicated, we would lose one of the few natural buffers to a potentially catastrophic change in climate.

MINERALS NEEDED BY RAIN-FOREST TREES

Rain-forest trees require 14 main mineral nutrients. Primary nutrients (P) are needed in large amounts; secondary nutrients (S) in medium amounts; and micronutrients (M) in minute quantities. All are essential for life.

NUTRIENT	ROLE
Nitrogen (P)	Needed for the formation of amino acids and DNA
Phosphorus (P)	Makes the chemical that stores energy in cells
Potassium (P)	Helps to regulate water and salts in and out of cells
Calcium (S)	Cell-wall formation, regulates plant response to light
Magnesium (S)	Component of chlorophyll, vital for photosynthesis
Sulphur (S)	Used in making proteins
Boron (M)	Helps form chlorophyll
Chloride (M)	Water regulation, and swelling and shrinking of cells
Copper (M)	Helps plants use proteins and helps root growth
Iron (M)	Component of enzymes used in photosynthesis
Manganese (M)	Aids production of oxygen from water
Molybdenum (M)	Helps with the production of amino acids
Nickel (M)	Involved in enzyme system that governs plant growth
Zinc (M)	Helps form chlorophyll

THUNDER AND LIGHTNING A violent electrical storm breaks over Brazil's Atlantic coast rain forest. Tropical rain forests experience the greatest frequency of thunderstorms, with storms sometimes occurring daily. The storms play a role in another vital cycle, the nitrogen cycle – lightning helps to convert nitrogen in the atmosphere into forms that can be used by living organisms.

THE FOREST'S ENGINE ROOM

THE SOIL IS A RAIN FOREST'S LIFE-SUPPORT SYSTEM. This is where dead and decaying plant and animal matter are turned back rapidly into new plants, especially trees. Yet most rain forests have surprisingly thin soils, partly because the processing time is so fast that useful materials remain in the soil for only a very short time. Minerals and nutrients are usually locked up in the trees, not the soils. If rain-forest trees are removed, the nutrients go with them, and without the trees, heavy rains can easily wash away what little soil is left. The result is a disruption in the natural cycle of decay and re-growth, and trees cannot grow again. It is the main reason why farmers who cut down the forest for agriculture can only grow crops or rear cattle for a short time before the soil is exhausted – at best one or two years.

Rain-forest soils are so acidic and nutrient-poor that more than two-thirds of rain forests worldwide – and about three-quarters of the Amazon Basin – are actually considered 'wet deserts'. The remaining forests are on fertile soils enriched from elsewhere. In the floodplain of the Amazon River, silt is brought down from the Andes, while on many islands in South-east Asia active volcanoes contribute new minerals.

Ancient soils

Rain-forest soils can be up to 100 million years old, which is another factor in the poverty of nutrients in most of them. In rain-forest basins, such as the Amazon, there has been little volcanic activity for millions of years, so most of their soils have

STRUCTURAL SUPPORT Many of the tallest rain-forest trees have huge buttress roots. These help to keep the trees standing in the thin soils and also absorb more nutrients than normal roots.

not been refreshed with nutrients. Topsoils tend to be exceedingly thin, little more than 2–5 cm deep. Over the centuries, rain has washed out essential plant minerals, such as phosphorus, potassium, calcium and magnesium, leaving behind aluminium oxide and iron oxide, which are useless to plants. These compounds are what give tropical soils their distinctive yellow or reddish colour.

Where soils are thin, tropical rain-forest trees have overcome the problem by having vast mats of shallow roots that spread out across the forest floor. The large surface area of these roots means that they can effectively absorb what little nutrients there are. The trees also have allies to help them to obtain the sustenance they need. Among their intricate network of roots lies an equally complex mass of branching, tendril-like filaments, called hyphae, which belong to fungi. These fungi – known as mycorrhizal fungi, from the Greek words for 'fungus' and 'root' – have formed a symbiotic relationship with the trees, in which they share their nutrients and water with the trees in return for sugars. The fungi's hyphae are even more efficient at collecting available nutrients than the trees' roots.

Soil-borne fungi like these are not unique to rain forests. They are thought to have developed in association with the earliest land plants and are essential for the evolution of land flora. More than 80 per cent of higher plants – ones with vascular tissue for transporting water, minerals and photosynthetic products around the plant – rely on fungi.

Staying upright

The long reach of rain-forest tree roots serves a structural purpose as well. The trees of the canopy are tall, and the topmost 'emergents', which poke above the canopy, are even taller. With the wet soils and strong winds that accompany tropical storms, shallow roots and great height could be a recipe for disaster. The trees have countered this with broad, rather than deep root systems that spread out in excess of 100 m from an individual tree. Emergents gain strength from sturdy buttress roots – large, vane-like extensions of the trunk that flare out about 6 m above the ground.

Other characteristics of rain-forest trees are also a result of their special environment. Their trunks tend to be straight with no branches below 30 m or more above the ground,

SPREADING ROOTS Smaller rain-forest trees have roots that are close to the surface and spread out over a considerable distance from the tree. They are tapping into nutrients in the topmost layers of the soil.

because the trees do not need branches and leaves where there is little or no light. Their bark is thin and smooth, partly because rain-forest trees do not have to cope with serious water loss or freezing. A smooth surface also helps to prevent plant parasites from getting a hold. In many rain-forest species, the bark of different trees is the same – a particular species can be identified only by its flowers.

With such high humidity, rot can be a problem for the taller trees, which rid themselves of excess water by having leaves with 'drip tips' to drain it away quickly. For the smaller plants living in the understorey, the situation is different. They often face a water and nutrient shortage and some species have developed so-called apogeotropic roots – from the Greek meaning 'turned away from the earth'. These fine, spindly roots

grow upwards along the trunks of their giant neighbours at a rate of 5.6 cm in three days. They can reach a height of 13 m, where they tap into nutrient-laden streams leached down from the canopy or rainwater running down the trunks.

Hangers on

As well as apogeotropic roots from neighbours, tall rain-forest trees tend to gather an increasing number of passengers as they grow older. Most of the burden comes from the masses of lianas and vines that crisscross the canopy and understorey. Their sheer weight can bring a rain-forest giant crashing to the ground. Yet these climbing plants can also have a helpful effect, because they anchor the trees together. An emergent, reaching the highest levels of the rain forest, is often held aloft by its lianas and neighbours in a huge tangle of vegetation. Trees may come and go, but the lianas and vines remain – some are up to 500 years old, which ranks them among the oldest plants in the forest.

Other hangers-on include a wealth of epiphytes (see page 56), such as orchids, bromeliads and ferns, which grow on branches in the canopy. Although these residents are not parasitic, excessive numbers can be a burden, overwhelming the tree. This has a simple system if things get out of hand – it self-prunes. It shuts down any branch overloaded with plants so that it withers and breaks off, sending the branch and its cargo of freeloading guests crashing to the forest floor.

RECYCLING THE NUTRIENTS

IN THE NEAR-UNCHANGING CLIMATE OF THE RAIN FOREST, TREES OF DIFFERENT SPECIES TEND TO SHED THEIR LEAVES AT DIFFERENT TIMES OF THE YEAR, and so leaves are constantly falling to the ground from one tree or another. A multitude of tiny creatures – the decomposers – get to work on this leaf litter, rapidly breaking it down. They also make good use of broken branches and dead flowers. Invertebrates, such as millipedes, giant cockroaches, beetles and colonies of termites, break up the larger pieces of deadwood; tackling things at a microscopic level are hosts of protozoans, bacteria, slime moulds, algae and fungi that thrive in warm, moist conditions. In some rain forests, giant earthworms – up to 2 m long – course through the leaf litter and soil.

Fruits and seeds falling from the canopy are mopped up immediately. Ground-living birds, such as the curassow of the South American rain forests, feed on the fruit pulp and seeds. Anything they miss is taken back by the forest itself. Tree roots

WASTE DISPOSAL As soon as dung drops to the forest floor, dung beetles are there in a flash, sometimes fighting over the choice pieces. They feed on the dung themselves or lay their eggs in it so emerging larvae have an instant food supply.

will even grow out of the ground and over a fallen fruit to take advantage of the temporary abundance. Fungal hyphae grow over an object in a matter of hours. They collect nutrients from rotting leaves, fruit and deadwood, breaking down the material into simple inorganic products that can be absorbed easily by the tree's roots or by mycorrhizal fungi in the soil. The entire process is extraordinarily rapid. Where a leaf may take a year to decompose in temperate woodland, it takes no more than six weeks in a tropical rain forest.

Feeding on waste

Nothing escapes recycling in the rain forest, where one animal's waste product is another creature's feast. Not even perspiration goes to waste. Sweat bees swarm around anything or anybody perspiring, taking advantage of the water and minerals contained in the sweat. Forest butterflies will even suck up the tears in the corners of the eyes of river turtles and caimans.

Butterflies also like dung. It is only a matter of minutes before newly dropped dung is discovered and covered with the brightly coloured insects, along with beetles and flies. They are not only attracted to the dung for its food value; it also contains important minerals, such as sodium and calcium. Skipper butterflies, with their big eyes, will respond to anything resembling a dollop of dung, even a white petal falling from a flower.

Male butterflies are generally more attracted than the females. They often pass on minerals to females they mate with to enhance their reproductive potential, and they obtain these minerals by 'puddling' in mud or dung. Occasionally, females join the males and puddle for themselves. There are even 'puddle clubs' in which several butterflies will feed on any excess fluid emanating

from each other as well as from the scat (animal faeces). They all join a procession of other dung lovers that follow monkeys, gibbons and any other creatures that drop their waste onto the forest floor. For their part, some species of monkey use their dung to deter intruders, and many a naturalist has looked up into the canopy, only to get one in the eye from a howler monkey perched overhead.

Dung wars

In the Amazon, within two minutes of woolly monkey scat hitting the ground, the dung beetles fly in. Male beetles fight for the best pieces, and then females lay their eggs in them. The beetles have competition in the form of a fly that lays its eggs in monkey scat, and down on the forest floor a battle rages between the two species. The maggots that hatch from the fly's eggs grow faster than the beetle grubs, but the dung beetles have a surprise ally. They carry a mite that is a parasite on the fly larvae. The mites feed on the fly larvae, leaving the young dung beetles with the scat all to themselves.

There are other insects that seek out dung, not for the excrement itself, but for the seeds it contains. Broad-headed bugs and seed

EXOTIC FUNGUS Fungi are only evident when their fruiting bodies push up through the soil, like this veiled fungus growing beside the fruits of a Michelia *tree in a Sri Lankan rain forest.*

bugs have barbed tips to their slender mandibles (mouthparts), which they use to cut through the outer covering of seeds. Having gained entrance, they pump in digestive enzymes that break down the body of the seed and then suck up the resulting soup.

And where there is dung, there are dung mimics. Most birds and mammals do not view dung as food, so to remain quite motionless, at least during the day, disguised as a dropping is advantageous to a small creature. Beetles, caterpillars, adult moths and even frogs do it. Predators do it, too. In the rain forests of South-east Asia, there is a crab spider that not only resembles a bird dropping but also spins a small, flat, white web resembling splashes of guano. Its artistry serves a deadly purpose, for it grabs any mineral-seeking insect that alights within reach of its fangs.

> **In the Amazon, within two minutes of woolly monkey scat hitting the ground the dung beetles fly in. Male beetles fight for the best pieces, and then females lay their eggs in them.**

TIMBER, FOOD AND MEDICINES

NEARLY 80 PER CENT OF OUR EVERYDAY FOODS HAVE THEIR ORIGINS IN RAIN FORESTS. While timber – such as ebony, teak, mahogany and balsa – is the best-known rain-forest product, the forests manufacture much more that is of benefit to humankind. Vegetables that originally grew in them include maize, potatoes, rice, winter squash and yams. Spices include black pepper, cayenne, cinnamon, cloves, ginger and turmeric. Sugar cane, chocolate, coffee, vanilla, Brazil nuts and cashews originate from the rain forest, as well as fruits such as avocados, figs, oranges, lemons, grapefruit, bananas, guavas, pineapples and mangos. In all, there are an extraordinary 3000 known rain-forest fruits. Of these, most of us eat only 200, but the forests' indigenous human inhabitants consume more than 2000 different types – and rain-forest animals exploit them all.

Tropical rain forests are also an important reservoir of natural medicines. Trees have been synthesising protective compounds, such as alkaloids, for millions of years. These protect them against leaf-eaters, infection, pests, and disease. They can also protect us against diseases. Already there are anaesthetics,

contraceptives, enzymes, hormones, laxatives, cough mixtures, antibiotics and antiseptics that have their origins in rain-forest species. Other derivatives from rain-forest plants are used to treat cancer, heart disease, malaria, tuberculosis, bronchitis, hypertension and dysentery. About 25 per cent of our medicines come from the rain forests, yet scientists have examined less than 5 per cent of known tropical rain-forest plants.

Forest secrets

The secrets of these medicines are well known to the forests' native inhabitants. Their natural pharmacopoeia is handed down from one generation to the next through oral history. In South-east Asia, for example, it is estimated that traditional healers use more than 6500 species of plants with known medical properties, and nearly 2 billion people across the region rely on rain-forest medicines to keep them healthy. In the Amazon, the number of medicinal plant species recorded so far is about 1300.

It was South America that gave us one of the first effective treatments for malaria – quinine, used by Westerners since the early 17th century. It is derived from the bark of the cinchona

UNSALTED NUTS Cashew nuts come from a small evergreen tree native to Brazil. The nut is actually a seed, which forms under a false fruit called the cashew apple. Left: Teak contains natural oils, making it durable without the need for treatment.

tree, which grows on the forested slopes of the Andes in places where the rainfall is high. Among local people, it was well known as a treatment against fevers. Its discovery for the Western world has been attributed to the region's Spanish *conquistadores* and the many priests who accompanied them – hence one of its early names, 'Jesuits' powder'. The most colourful story involves the Countess of Chinchón, wife of a Spanish viceroy of Peru, who contracted malaria in 1638. She was given the powdered bark, which was sometimes mixed with lemon juice, and recovered. Some time later, the naturalist Carolus Linnaeus named the tree in her honour, but spelled it wrongly, so the scientific name of the 25 species of shrubs and trees became *Cinchona* species.

Today in north-western Brazil, isolated tribes use forest plants to treat fungal infections, snakebites and insect stings and to shift internal parasites and relieve aches and pains. Initially, their healers had few treatments against Western diseases, but even that has changed. After contact with the outside world, healers have introduced new medicines, indicating that their experiments with the medicinal properties of rain-forest plants have continued. It is from pools of local knowledge like these that Western pharmaceutical companies expect to find new products to fight diseases in the 21st century.

Multi-purpose medicines

Many plants turn out to be useful against more than one condition. The chilli pepper is used traditionally both to soothe upset stomachs and, when mixed into an ointment, to relieve arthritis. Physostigmine and neostygmine are two drugs derived from the Calabar bean of West Africa, which has been used for some time to treat glaucoma and is now being explored as a treatment for Alzheimer's disease.

Researchers have identified nearly 3000 plants that have compounds active against cancers, and three-quarters of them are from rain forests. Some

CANCER AID Although widely cultivated for decorative as well as medical purposes, Madagascar's rosy periwinkle is endangered in the wild due to loss of its rain-forest habitat.

are proving effective. Vincristine from Madagascar's rosy periwinkle is used to treat childhood leukaemia. One shadow over the discovery has been the fact that the local people of Madagascar received little remuneration for their knowledge. Pharmaceutical companies are coming under increasing criticism for exploiting native peoples in this way.

One method that avoids this is 'text mining' – visiting libraries and examining the many books written over the centuries by travellers and settlers for references to medicinal plants. One source has been *The Ambonese Herbal*, a record of 1300 plant species native to South-east Asia, compiled by the German botanist, Georg Everhard Rumph, in the 17th century. He was working with the Dutch East India Company on the island of Ambon in Indonesia and began collecting the information because of the delay in receiving medicines from Europe. He wrote seven volumes of ethno-medical records, a valuable resource that is being examined today by pharmacologists.

RAIN-FOREST MEDICINES

Products from the rain forests are already widely used in medicine, from fighting leukaemia and HIV to birth control to treating skin conditions, such as psoriasis.

PLACE OF ORIGIN	PLANT	SUBSTANCE	USES
Madagascar	Rosy periwinkle	Vincristine/vinblastine	Childhood leukaemia, Hodgkin's disease
Brazil (Amazon)	Araroba tree	Dithranol	Psoriasis
Borneo	Mangosteen family	Calanolide A	HIV
Mexico	Mexican yam	Diosgenin	Birth control pill
Cameroon	*Ancistrocladus korupensis* (liana)	Michellamine B	HIV
Brazil	Curare vine	Tubocuarine	Muscle relaxant
Africa	*Aspilia* species	Thiaubrine	Antibiotic
India	Indian snakeroot	Reserpine	High blood pressure
Africa	Calabar bean	Neostigmine	Glaucoma

TEMPERATE RAIN FORESTS

RAIN FORESTS ARE NOT CONFINED TO THE TROPICS. They can be found wherever there is enough moisture in the air for almost year-round rainfall and temperatures are suitable for tree growth. These conditions can occur in temperate regions, including parts of Europe and North America, where strips of land lie next to the ocean and are backed by mountain ranges. The forests that grow there, called temperate rain forests, contain fewer tree species than their tropical counterparts, but the trees they have are often enormous, including some of the largest anywhere in the world.

One such strip of rain forest lies along the north-western coast of North America, where trees reach record-breaking proportions. Their giant size is a result of geography and climate. Moist air blowing in from the Pacific rises above the mountain ranges that line the coast and becomes trapped by them. It condenses and falls as heavy rain. These conditions, in which mild, wet winters are followed by cool, foggy summers, support a series of rain forests, from the sitka spruce forests of south-western Alaska as far south as the redwood forests of northern California. Time there appears to go more slowly than in the rest of the world, and many of the trees have stood for thousands of years.

Land of giants

The redwoods and sequoias of California's temperate rain forests include some of the greatest trees on the planet. Several have been given their own names, such as General Sherman in the Sequoia National Park. This majestic tree is the world's largest by volume – 83.8 m high (as tall as some 20-storey buildings), with a diameter of 9 m at the base and calculated to have a volume of 1489 m^3. Its main trunk alone is estimated to weigh in excess of 2000 tonnes. At around 2200 years old, General Sherman is a comparative youngster as sequoias go, and it is still growing – it adds enough wood each year to make a tree 30 m tall and 30 cm in diameter.

Other redwoods and sequoias are more than 3500 years old, which is middle-aged for temperate rain-forest trees. The oldest known redwood still standing – Eternal God in the Prairie Creek Redwoods State Park, California – is thought to be between 7000 and 12 000 years old. Many trees that have reached old age have already toppled over, including the largest by volume ever measured – the Lindsey Creek Tree, a coastal redwood from north-western California, with a trunk volume of more than 2500 m^3 and a mass of 3630 tonnes. It was blown over by high winds in a violent storm in 1905. The tallest living tree is thought to be another coastal redwood, the Mendocino Tree in Montgomery State Reserve, which is 112 m tall. It is estimated to be around 1000 years old – no more than a baby in redwood terms.

Record-breaking fungus

North of California, Douglas firs, sitka spruces, cedars and western hemlocks dominate the rain forests of Oregon and Washington states. Vine maple and dogwoods form the understorey, while thimbleberries, huckleberries, sword ferns and Oregon grape plants

VEILED GIANTS Fog shrouds a redwood forest in northern California's Marin County. High levels of humidity help to create the conditions in which temperate rain forests can thrive.

FACTS

2000 RAIN-FOREST TREES ARE CUT DOWN EVERY MINUTE.

Yet only one tree is replanted for every ten cut down. It is thought that 50 species are disappearing every day due to deforestation, and with only 5 per cent of forests protected as nature reserves or national parks, we could lose the rest within 200 years.

6 PER CENT of the world's land surface is covered by rain forests, yet they account for 50 per cent of its biodiversity.

THE OLDEST RAIN FORESTS ARE IN MALAYSIA.

They may have been there for 100 million years.

FACTS

inhabit the forest floor. A Douglas fir that once grew on Washington State's Olympic Peninsula was another of the world's tallest trees – some 128 m high. Nowadays, the region's most impressive record-holders lie largely hidden from view. Below the forest floor in the Blue Mountains of eastern Oregon is the largest-known living organism on Earth – a colony of honey mushrooms, spanning an area of 8.9 km^2, the equivalent of 1220 football pitches, and weighing an estimated 600 tonnes. A similar colony is growing near Mount Adams in Washington State.

The honey mushroom attacks the sapwood of trees, growing under the bark as a mass of fine fungal strands called mycelia or across the ground between trees as dark root-like structures called rhizomorphs or 'shoestrings'. The rhizomorphs are able to carry nutrients and water over long distances and behave as scouts, seeking out new trees to invade. Most of the fungus's activity is hidden inside the trees or underground. Above ground, scatterings of edible mushroom-like fruiting bodies push up from time to time and are among the few visible signs that it is there at all.

With such enormous trees and other organisms, it is not surprising that temperate rain forests are more densely packed with materials of a biological origin than any other habitat in the

Below the forest floor in the Blue Mountains of eastern Oregon is the largest-known living organism on Earth – a colony of honey mushrooms, weighing an estimated 600 tonnes.

world, including tropical rain forests. Botanists have estimated that the rain forests of North America's Pacific North-West have a biomass of between 1000 and 5000 tonnes per hectare.

A world of rain forests

Other temperate rain forests lie scattered across the globe. There are stands in the Appalachian Mountains of eastern North America. In South America, the Valdivian forests of southern Chile spread out along a narrow strip of land between the Andes and the Pacific and on the offshore islands of Chiloé and the Chronos Archipelago. Dominating the Valdivian forests are southern beeches, laurel-leaved trees, monkey puzzles and alerces. The sequoia-like alerce rivals some North American trees for longevity – a few specimens are thought to be more than 3625 years old. Animals present in the Valdivian forests include the monito del monte, a small tree-living marsupial, and the kodkod, a small wild cat.

The Magellanic sub-polar rain forest lies at the southernmost tip of Chile and Argentina and on the island

IN THE NORTH Alaska's temperate rain forests (shown in dark green) stretch in a 1600 km arc along the Pacific coast and include Tongass and Chugach National Forests.

NORTHERN TEMPERATE

of Tierra del Fuego. Its main trees are southern beeches, and the forest floor harbours delicious fruits, such as the Chilean strawberry and the calafate or Magellan barberry, both used locally to make jams. The forest is home to the world's smallest deer, the pudú, standing just 40 cm tall at the shoulder, while Magellanic penguins nest among the tree roots close to the seashore. Together, the Magellanic and Valdivian forests make up the world's second largest temperate rain forests.

There are more rain forests on the remote island of Tristan da Cuhna in the South Atlantic, and South Africa has the Knysna-Amatole Forest on the southern slopes of the Drakensberg mountains. Fogs from the Indian Ocean frequently cloak the Knysna-Amatole Forest, whose trees include ironwoods, stinkwoods and several species of podocarps – southern conifers, such as the real yellowwood. The forest was also home to the most southerly elephant population in Africa, although their numbers have now dwindled to the point where no more than a couple of individuals survive.

Southern beeches and podocarps grow in the west coast rain forests of New Zealand's South Island, and southern beeches, together with King Billy pines and Huon pines, are characteristic of rain forests on Tasmania's west coast. In Australia, temperate rain forests also occur in parts of Victoria, New South Wales and southern Queensland. Japan has rain forests in the Kirishima-Yaku National Park on Kyushu island as well as in Yoshino-Kumano National Park on Honshu island.

In Taiwan, rain forests occur in the eastern part of the island and on the slopes of the central mountains.

The south-eastern shore of the Black Sea has the Colchian forests of Turkey and Georgia, where the rainfall is in excess of 1000 mm a year. Trees that thrive there include alders, hornbeams, oriental beeches and Europe's largest trees – Nordmann firs, which reach heights of 78 m. In Britain, remnant rain forests, with oak and birch as the dominant species, still stand in the Scottish Highlands – at Taynish and Crinan woods, near Lochgilphead and Glasdrum, between Oban and Fort William. The forest at Taynish is at least 7000 years old, and the relatively mild, moist climate supports a rich oceanic fern, bryophyte and lichen community. It is also home to the very rare marsh fritillary butterfly.

All across the world, the size of many trees in temperate rain forests and their local abundance make them valuable commercially. Like their tropical counterparts, they have often been cut down for timber, and as a result, more than half of all the world's temperate rain forests have already gone. Much of the rest, such as Great Bear Rain Forest on Canada's western seaboard – the largest surviving unbroken tract of temperate rain forest in the world – is threatened.

IN THE SOUTH Cool temperate rain forests (dark green) cover 10 per cent of Tasmania. They are home to the Tasmanian devil, the world's largest marsupial carnivore.

SOUTHERN TEMPERATE

THE BAT
FOR LI

TLE GHT

2

MIST SHROUDS THE ECUADORIAN RAIN FOREST (LEFT), WHERE UP TO 300 SPECIES OF TREE CAN BE FOUND IN JUST ONE HECTARE OF FOREST. For the millions of plants living in a closely packed rain forest, every day is a battle for light. Trees grow fast, their trunks extending upwards, straight and bare, until they reach the canopy, where they branch out to catch the light while blocking it from other plants below. The many plants living in the rain forest have developed different strategies for capturing whatever light is available, and this has stratified rain forests into clearly defined zones: the forest floor, understorey, canopy and overstorey. Animals living in the rain forest are for the most part hidden from view, each species occupying its own place in the forest's vertical structure.

FOREST LEVELS

Every living thing in a tropical rain forest has its particular place, or niche, in one of the layers of vegetation between the ground and the treetops. The rain forest has four basic layers. The overstorey consists of the tops of the tallest, or emergent, trees. The canopy is where most leaves and most rain-forest life is found. In the understorey, small trees and shrubs struggle for light. The shrub layer and forest floor harbour the bacteria, fungi and insects that recycle the constant supply of plant and animal material raining down from the layers above.

Height above ground

60 m

FOREST SENTINEL The harpy eagle of South and Central America uses the tallest trees in the rain forest as a lookout post to spot the movement of prey in the canopy. The eagle's short wings enable it to manoeuvre through the trees.

HANGING AROUND During the day, fruit bats, or flying foxes, hang upside down on the branches of the tallest trees, where they are safe from most predators. At dusk they fly off in search of fruit, their huge numbers often blacking out the sky.

OVERSTOREY

The trees that push up into the overstorey receive the most light, but are also buffeted by wind, lashed by rain and are vulnerable to lightning strikes during electrical storms.

IRIDESCENT BLUE Scales on the wings of the morpho butterfly of South and Central America reflect light in such a way that the wings seem to change colour when viewed from different angles.

50 m

SEE-THROUGH FROGS Glass frogs are lime green on their backs but have translucent skin on their bellies, revealing their internal organs. They live among the trees of the canopy, close to water.

CANOPY

This is where all the food for the rain forest is manufactured. The leaves photosynthesise rapidly, and trees have a high yield of fruit, shoots, berries, nuts and seeds.

40 m

CANOPY NEIGHBOURS

The tropical rain-forest canopy is a mosaic of leaves and branches, yet rarely do trees interlock or actually touch. Each is separated from its neighbour by a few feet. This prevents pest species, such as leaf-eating caterpillars, and diseases spreading from one tree to the next, but it also means that rain-forest animals must be able to leap, glide or fly across the gaps. The diademed sifaka of Madagascar, for example, can leap across gaps up to 9 m wide, thrusting itself from one treetrunk to the next at a take-off speed of 30 km/h.

MONKEY STAND-IN The marsupial cuscuses of Australia and New Guinea are nocturnal omnivores that hunt in the canopy and understorey. They occupy a similar ecological niche to forest monkeys in other parts of the world.

TOP PREDATOR The jaguar of South and Central America hunts at all levels between the floor and the canopy, and will even swim. Its spotted coat renders it almost invisible, helping it to surprise its prey.

INSECT-CATCHER
The brown gerygone spends much of its time in the understorey, but hunts insects at all levels in Queensland's rain forests. It catches them on leaves and branches, and will also take them in flight.

UNDERSTOREY

Very little sunlight breaks through the mosaic of leaves in the canopy, so plants and animals living in the understorey are adapted to functioning at low light levels.

FOREST FLOOR

Plant and animal material decomposes and provides nutrients for insects in the leaf litter and for the forest's fast-growing trees.

30 m

20 m

10 m

0 m

WITH ONLY TWO PER CENT OF AVAILABLE SUNLIGHT FILTERING DOWN THROUGH THE DENSE CANOPY, THE TROPICAL RAIN-FOREST FLOOR IS DARK DAY AND NIGHT. Contrary to popular belief, there is no tangle of jungle at ground level, just leaf litter, moss-covered logs and branches, decaying fruit, lichens and fungi. Hidden away in this shady, humid world are myriad tiny creatures, including cockroaches, crickets, beetles, scorpions, spiders, centipedes, millipedes and tiny frogs. Many feed on the decaying plant and animal matter that has fallen to the ground, and are themselves food for larger animals, such as snakes, lizards and small mammals. Forest-floor reptiles are well camouflaged. The tiny brown chameleon of central African rain forests, for example, looks like a leaf, and even its tail, which is flat rather than coiled and tapers to a point, is like the tip of a leaf.

Forest foragers

Fallen fruits and nuts do not last long on the Amazon forest floor; they provide food for agoutis by day and pacas at night. Tapirs, with their long flexible snouts, forage for tubers under the ground, while bands of peccaries snuffle about, eating just about anything that is edible. All are vulnerable to predators such as jaguars and harpy eagles. Tapirs are also found in the rain forests of southern Asia, where they are known as the *mu-nam*, meaning 'water pig'. They have poor eyesight, but excellent hearing and sense of smell to help them in the gloomy world they inhabit. Deer, bearded pigs and moon rats join them on the ground, and their main predator is the tiger.

The grubs and insects that inhabit the leaf litter provide good pickings for birds. Rain forests in New Guinea and Queensland are populated by the white-tailed paradise kingfisher, log-runners and chowchillas, whose loud calls are part of the rain-forest dawn chorus. They are joined by the duet of the male and female whipbird, the male performing the whip-crack, the most characteristic sound of the Australian rain forest, and the female following with a quick 'choo-choo'. At night, the birds are replaced by marsupials, such as the long-nosed bandicoot, which pushes its long, pointed snout into holes it has dug with its forefeet. When it finds food it grunts with satisfaction.

HIDDEN DANGER The gaboon viper of West Africa is hard to spot in the leaf litter on the forest floor. It has the longest fangs and delivers the most venom of any snake.

MIDNIGHT FEAST The paca of South America searches at night for fruit that has fallen to the ground.

FOREST FLOOR

LONG FACE The aptly named bearded pig inhabits forests of Malaysia and Indonesia, where its diet includes fruit, worms and roots. It often follows troops of monkeys to pick up fruit that they drop to the ground.

UNDERSTOREY

THE RAIN-FOREST UNDERSTOREY, LIKE THE FLOOR, IS DARK ALL THE TIME. NO MORE THAN FIVE PER CENT OF SUNLIGHT PENETRATES HERE. Plant species living at this level have adaptations that enable them to gather every photon of available light. Many have dark green leaves packed with chlorophyll for converting sunlight into energy, and some have leaves that rotate to follow the Sun. A few will be familiar since understorey plants, such as the Swiss cheese plant from Central America, make good houseplants as they thrive in the warm ambient temperatures of our homes and are adapted to low light levels.

Climbing towards the light

Many of the plants that inhabit the understorey are climbers that twist from the floor right up to the canopy. There are climbing versions of many plant groups, including climbing palms, climbing ferns and even the climbing gymnosperm *Gnetum*, which is found in rain forests across the world. In Indonesia, flour ground from the plant's seeds is used to make the bitter-tasting crackers that accompany local dishes.

The most obvious climbers are the woody lianas. This is not a species in itself, but is a general term for fast-climbing rain-forest plants that, although not parasites, rely on other trees for support. There are 2500 known species from 90 families of vines, and there are so many individual plants criss-crossing the understorey that they account for up to 10 per cent of above-ground vegetation. Lianas have a slightly different internal structure to other plants. They carry more water in their stems

CAMPING OUT Tent-making bats take shelter under a palm leaf (above). They fold the broad palm leaf together by biting and weakening the main midrib so that the sides flop down, providing the bats with a safe roosting site.

KILLER GRIP The tight embrace of the strangler fig (right) will eventually kill the tall host tree that supports it.

and assign fewer nutrients to supporting tissues, using all the energy to grow leaves, roots and an exceptionally long stem, which can reach up to 900 m long. Their structure gives them flexibility, enabling them to grow rapidly in both vertical and horizontal directions. In fact, many grow as long outwards as they do upwards on their convoluted journey to the canopy in search of the life-giving sunlight. The intertwined vines create natural highways that not only bridge the gaps between trees, but also provide ladders between the different forest layers. Some vines are strong enough to support a jaguar, or even a human giving tree-dwelling animals greater mobility through the forest and increasing their foraging or hunting potential.

Rain-forest strangler

One plant that has taken the notion of 'support' to a sinister extreme is the strangler fig. Its survival strategy in the rain forest is to overwhelm and then eliminate any competition, which it achieves in the most underhand way. A seed lodges in soil trapped, say, in the fork of a large tree. The seed sends out aerial roots that grow down to the ground. The roots thicken and

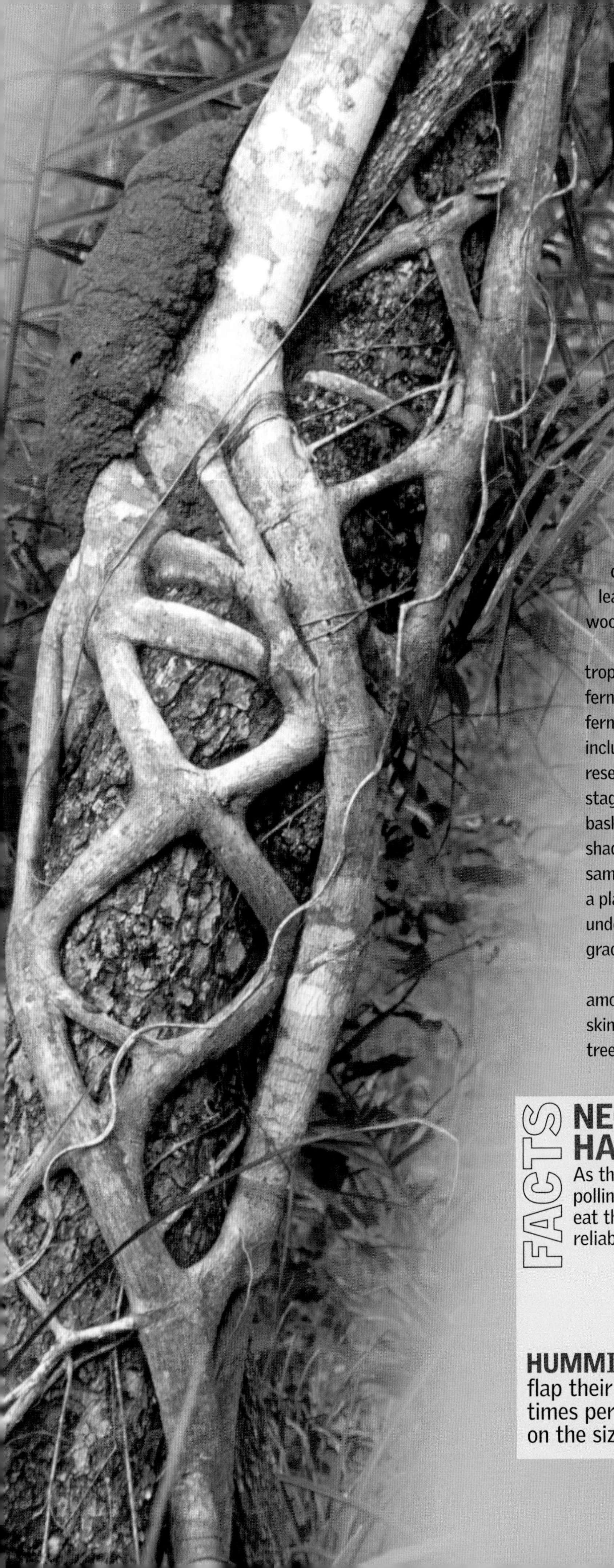

As the host tree grows
and expands it pushes
against the strangler
fig's roots. Eventually
the rain-forest giant
dies, having effectively
been strangled to death.

become woody, the substantial root network eventually encasing the tree. As the host tree grows and expands, it pushes against the strangler fig's roots. These restrict the host tree's inner vessels (known as phloem), preventing nutrients and water from reaching its branches and leaves. Eventually, the rain-forest giant dies, having effectively been strangled to death by its invader. The dead tree then slowly disintegrates, leaving the fig standing in its place, the old tree's decaying wood providing nutrients for the sneaky fig.

The understorey is also populated by many types of tropical fern. In Queensland's rain forests there are ground-living ferns, tree ferns and, on branches below the canopy, epiphytic ferns that form miniature forests in themselves. Common species include the bird's-nest fern with its large, crinkled leaves that resemble banana leaves, the deeply lobed elkhorn fern and staghorn fern, which look something like a stag's antlers, and basket ferns with feather-like fronds. Many orchids prefer the shadier conditions below the leaf layer, too. They all have the same basic structure of three petals, with one larger one forming a platform to support visiting bees and butterflies. Palms are also understorey plants, with the Atherton and majestic palms gracing Australian forests at an elevation above 800 m.

Insects, such as cicadas, crickets and stick insects, hide amongst the understorey foliage, where they fall prey to geckos, skinks and small birds, such as robins, fantails, scrubwrens and treecreepers. Tropical pigeons and bowerbirds nest at this level,

FACTS

NECTAR-FEEDING BATS HAVE HAIRS THAT COLLECT POLLEN.
As they move from flower to flower they provide a pollination service. When the bats groom themselves they eat the pollen grains from their hair. Pollen is the bats' only reliable source of nitrogen.

IN SOME FORESTS 70 PER CENT OF FRUIT-EATERS depend on figs for their survival.

HUMMINGBIRDS flap their wings 50–200 times per second, depending on the size of the bird.

FACTS

the female bowerbird bringing up her offspring alone while the male spends the breeding season attracting other females to his elaborately constructed bower on the forest floor.

Understorey pollinators

There is little or no wind in the understorey so plants must rely on insects, birds and bats for pollination. In the Amazon, delicate and colourful hummingbirds hover in front of flowers. They get their energy by feeding on sugary nectar and obtain protein from catching small insects. The hummingbirds, which are active during the day, are attracted to flowers by their bright colours and showy blooms, but at dusk a different type of nectar-feeding pollinator takes over.

Between 5.30 and 6.30 each evening, some flowers start to produce exceptionally powerful perfumes with the aim of attracting the night pollinators – moths and bats.

Flowers that give off a heavy scent, whether during the day or at night, are not situated at the points of new growth among the branches, but on the trunk of the tree, an arrangement known as 'cauliflory'. Flowers in this position are more easily accessed by larger pollinators, such as birds, bats and climbing mammals. Species of calabash tree (not to be confused with the calabash vine), found in Central and South America, have flowers on their stems that bloom at night, attracting bats.

The cannonball tree relies on bees for pollination and it gives its insect friends a special incentive to visit. The tree is a close relative of the Brazil nut and native to the Amazon, although it has been planted in forests around the world. It has scented orange, dark red or pink flowers growing on its trunk, each with two types of stamen. A ring of stamens produces fertile pollen, while another group of stamens produces infertile pollen that is a gift from the tree to the bee.

When the flowers fade, woody ball-shaped fruits grow in their place. They resemble small clusters of cannonballs on stalks, hence the tree's common name. As the fruits fall and hit the ground they break open, revealing small seeds set in a white jelly, which turns blue-green when exposed to the air. It smells unpleasant, but peccaries are attracted by the aroma. They eat the pulp, the seeds pass through the gut and are deposited on the ground, complete with a dollop of fertiliser to kick-start germination.

The sapucaia or paradise nut, another relative of the Brazil nut, has a similar pollination incentive for bees, but its seeds are dispersed with the help of bats. The fruit is about the size of a human head and has a hatch on its underside that drops away when the seeds are ready. The seeds are packed together, each attached to the inner fruit wall by a cord, or funicle, surrounded by a white, fleshy aril (a false fruit). The hard outer fruit protects the seeds, and as soon as the hatch opens, bats tear out the seeds and fly back to their roost. They eat the aril and drop the seeds onto the ground, where some may germinate.

It all seems foolproof, but the paradise nut tree did not count on brown capuchin monkeys. These South American monkeys have worked out how to open the fruit's hatch and eat the seeds before they are ripe. Researchers monitoring a single tree visited by capuchins found that a troop of these seed predators can destroy 99.5 per cent of its entire seed production.

READY TO DROP The large spherical fruits of the cannonball tree grow from flowers that bloom in clusters on the trunk rather than the branches. This gives easier access to pollinators.

THE SLOTH IS PERFECTLY ADAPTED TO

ARBOREAL LIVING – IT EATS, SLEEPS, MATES AND EVEN GIVES BIRTH WHILE HANGING UPSIDE DOWN FROM THE BRANCH OF A TREE. Its limbs are equipped with long, curved claws for hanging from branches using little energy: sloths have been found still hanging under branches after death. The sloth feeds mainly on leaves, but this is a poor food and difficult to digest, so it has a multi-chambered stomach, each chamber containing bacteria to break down the plant-cell walls and release the nutrients inside. The sloth stuffs itself with leaves, together with a few tender shoots and buds and the occasional insect, then sleeps for up to 18 hours while its stomach sets to work. It may rest in a sitting position in the fork of a tree, but more often it simply hangs upside down. Some stay in the same tree for many years – only moving on when the supply of leaves is exhausted. Young sloths cling to their mother's fur.

The sloth has fewer muscles than other mammals of similar size, so its progress is very slow, no more than 30 cm per minute in the trees, 1.5 m per minute on the ground and a sedate 4.5 m per minute when in a hurry. This languid rate of movement not only conserves energy, it also helps the sloth to avoid drawing attention to itself. Its brown fur gives it good camouflage, augmented by blue-green algae living in its hair, giving its fur a green tinge. Its coat plays host to a moth that has wings but rarely flies. If the sloth needs to swim, any resident moths perch on its head. When the sloth comes down to the base of a tree to defecate, the moths lay their eggs in the droppings, which the emerging caterpillars will later feed on. When the sloth has finished, the moths clamber back on board and the party returns to the trees.

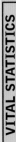
CLASS: Mammalia

ORDER: Pilosa

SPECIES: *Bradypus* spp. and *Choloepus* spp.

DISTRIBUTION: Central and South America

KEY FEATURE: Slow-moving mammal that lives in rain-forest trees and feeds on leaves

SLOTH

NATURE'S POWERS

CANOPY

SEEN FROM BELOW, THE CROWNS OF TREES AND THEIR BRANCHES SPREAD OUT IN EVERY DIRECTION, LIKE GREAT UMBRELLAS OF LEAVES. They form an almost solid ceiling – the canopy – up to 45 m above the ground and as much as 15 m thick, blocking out almost all the light from the forest below. Trees stand close together, but their branches rarely intertwine with those of their neighbours – a system possibly designed to prevent disease or plagues of leaf-eating insects, such as caterpillars, from spreading. Leaves tend to be small, green and waxy, an adaptation for retaining water. Each leaf is a sophisticated photochemical factory, converting water and carbon dioxide into sugars that the tree uses to grow. While decomposition and recycling take place on the ground, the canopy is where food is manufactured. It is the basis for the entire rain-forest ecosystem.

There are so many leaves, flowers and nuts and so much fruit that animals living in the canopy need never touch the ground. In the Amazon, many species of monkeys take advantage of what the trees have to offer. Troops of chattering uakaris, for example, travel between the topmost branches of the canopy and rarely visit the forest floor. They have sharp teeth and powerful jaws that enable them to eat hard, unripe fruits, gaining a head start on other fruit-eaters

BIRD'S-EYE VIEW High above the shady forest floor, a preying mantis reflects the Sun as it waits to ambush passing prey in the canopy of a Panamanian rain forest.

HEADS UP Tall trees rise out of the rain-forest canopy in Sabah, Borneo. There can be more tree species in a small tract of forest here than in the whole of North America.

and avoiding a mad scramble when fruit is ripe. The red uakari, as its name suggests, has a red face, a sign of good health but a complexion that has earned the monkey the nickname 'Englishman' on account of its resemblance to a red-faced colonial.

Subterfuge in the canopy

Colour for camouflage is important for the smaller canopy inhabitants. Many insects, including stick insects, leaf-insects, katydids (a type of grasshopper), leaf-hoppers and mantids, have developed extraordinary body structures and colours to mimic the flowers, leaves and twigs over which they clamber. There are species that mimic dead and living leaves, half-eaten leaves, twigs, bark, thorns, flowers and even bird droppings. Some are predators wanting to surprise their prey, while others are prey hiding from animals that want to eat them. Giant walking-stick insects from western Malaysia and Borneo are among the latter. They are the world's longest insects, with female specimens reaching 55 cm with their legs outstretched.

Mimicry is not confined to insects. Some plants do it, too. A few passionflower species have evolved a way to fool butterflies. Heliconid butterflies like to lay their eggs on passionflowers, and to dissuade them from doing so the plant has tapped into the butterfly's egg-laying behaviour. Female butterflies avoid laying their eggs on plants already visited by other females. So, the passionflower produces tiny, oval, yellow swellings that resemble butterfly eggs. It even produces them in the right place – at the tips of tendrils. Any butterfly coming along sees the false eggs and, believing it has arrived too late, flies to another plant. In this way the passionflower limits the number of caterpillars consuming its leaves.

One plant – the piranha tree of the Amazon – has taken this relationship with insects to an extreme, accommodating the insect's destructive behaviour. At the peak of the flood season, moth caterpillars feed on the leaves, almost stripping the tree bare. The caterpillars then pupate, and the tree quickly grows a second crop of leaves that goes untouched. The new leaves manufacture the sugars needed to produce flowers, by which time adult moths emerge from the pupae and pollinate the flowers.

Giant rain-forest butterflies

Some of the most spectacular moths and butterflies in the world are found in the rain-forest canopy. The largest is Queen Alexandria's birdwing butterfly, an appropriate name as it has a 30 cm wingspan and looks more like a bird than a butterfly. It is found in northern New Guinea, as is the world's second-largest butterfly, the goliath birdwing, with a wingspan of 28 cm. Males have black, yellow and green wings and they pursue the slightly larger but duller females through the canopy using a powerful flight. The chase may take them high over the canopy, followed by a sudden dive into the canopy to mate.

Malaysia's king of butterflies is Rajah Brooke's birdwing, the males having unusually long, narrow wings reminiscent of a glider, and Australia's largest is the Cairns birdwing, with a 16 cm wingspan. The upper side of its wings are mainly black with emerald green flashes. South America's contenders are the blue morpho, several species of butterfly with a wingspan up to 20 cm. The males have iridescent blue wings, and they frequently drink the juice of decaying fruit, using their long proboscis like a straw. Many morphos will fly together and, like birds, they mob animals that might prey upon them.

AGILE LIZARD The green iguana is a good tree climber. If danger threatens, it will drop out of the canopy and crash to the ground unharmed.

NIGHTLIFE

THE RAIN FOREST NEVER SLEEPS. DURING THE NIGHT THE CANOPY IS ALIVE WITH CREATURES MAKING THE MOST OF THE RELATIVE SAFETY OF DARKNESS. Some 30 m up in the Amazon canopy are the world's only nocturnal monkeys. The night, or owl, monkeys spend the night feeding mainly on ripe fruits, with a supplement of young leaves, insects and birds' eggs. Their unusually large eyes give them excellent night vision, and they can grab flying insects, such as moths, from mid-air.

A nocturnal lifestyle is more usually associated with more primitive primates, such as the lorises. In Borneo, the slow loris is active at night. Like the sloth, the loris is a slow mover, but its grasping hands have opposable thumbs and it is an accomplished climber. With slow, deliberate movements it creeps up on insects, frogs and lizards, grabbing them suddenly with a lightning catch.

Night is also the domain of magnificent moths, the three largest being the white witch, Atlas and Hercules moths of South-east Asia and Australia. Males and females find each other in the darkness using chemical messengers, or pheromones, which females waft through the air. Males have feathery antennae that can pick up the scent of just a few molecules from several kilometres away.

WINGED GIANT The Atlas moth (right) has wings up to 30 cm across with a surface area of 400 cm^2 – the largest of any known moth.

SLOW BUT SURE The loris creeps up on its prey, its large eyes so perfectly adapted for night vision that it can pluck an insect from the air.

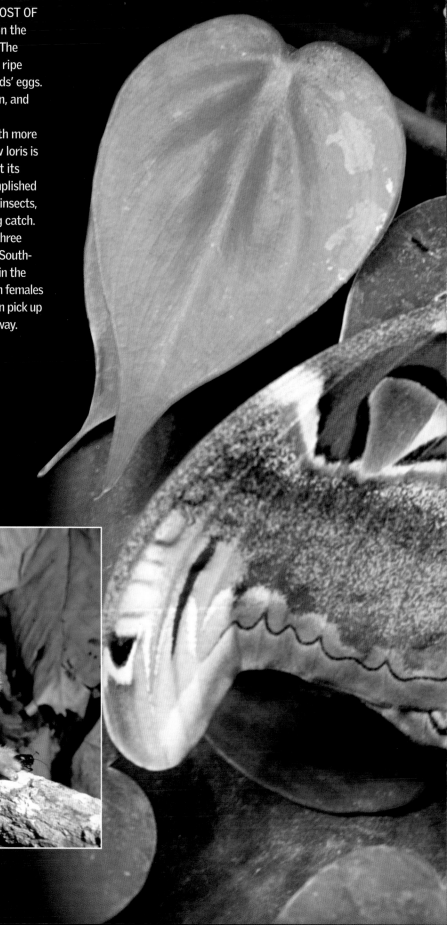

HANGING GARDENS

WHILE THE STRAIGHT, SMOOTH TRUNKS OF RAIN-FOREST TREES ARE CLEAR OF ANY HANGERS-ON, BRANCHES UP IN THE CANOPY CAN BE FESTOONED WITH A GREAT VARIETY OF 'AIR PLANTS', OR EPIPHYTES. A tree might be host to green mats of mosses, drooping beard-like lichens, feathery ferns, spiky-leaved bromeliads and beautiful flowering orchids. The plants use the tree for support, forming miniature gardens in its branches, but they do not tap into the tree for food. They are simply trying to gain a place in the Sun, and there might be as many as 2000 epiphytes on a single tree.

Not being rooted in soil, an epiphyte's main problem is to obtain water and nutrients, and many have adaptations more usually associated with desert plants. Dew, moisture in the air and water running down the host tree are the main sources of water. Orchids extract moisture from the humid atmosphere through dead cells, known as the velamen, on the outside of their roots. The staghorn fern has two types of leaf: broad leaves with overlapping margins that form an open funnel to collect water, and dark green, narrow leaves for photosynthesis. Mosses and lichens dry up when water is scarce, but absorb it quickly and continue to grow when it is available again. Having acquired water the plant must retain it, and many epiphytes have small, waxy leaves to reduce water loss. Orchids generally store water in plump leaves and bulbous stems, while bromeliads have reservoirs formed from their rosette of stiff overlapping leaves.

Nutrients are available from a variety of sources. Epiphytes can absorb them from dust washed from the host tree's leaves and from dead leaves trapped in its branches. Staghorn and bird's-nest ferns in South-east Asia trap debris among their fronds and send out roots to tap into any soil that has accumulated. Orchids trap plant debris in a lattice of aerial roots. They also have a symbiotic relationship with mycorrhizal fungi, which break down the materials more effectively than the orchid, providing the plant with additional nutrients. Some epiphytes even employ the help of insects. In South-east Asia, for example, so-called ant plants have swollen bases to their stems and chambers that provide homes for ants.

The ants benefit from the shelter provided by the plant, and the plant benefits from any materials brought in by the ants. The ants also protect the plants from leaf-eating insects. Epiphytes provide microhabitats in the canopy for a variety of other creatures, including earthworms and giant planarians (flatworms). These crawl through the canopy system, processing the decaying plant matter in which the epiphytes are growing. Even leeches are found up here.

Making more epiphytes

Epiphytes reproduce in much the same way as other plants, with colourful flowers attracting pollinators, whether these be insects, bats or birds. Orchids have developed special one-to-one relationships, certain species producing a flower and scent designed to lure in a specific insect pollinator. The resulting minute seeds are carried on air currents through the canopy. Those that land in a suitable place, such as the fork of a tree, will begin the cycle again.

CLOSER TO THE LIGHT Epiphytes festoon a tree branch in the Australian rain forest, creating a rain forest in miniature high up in the canopy. Many orchids take advantage of the better light supply in the canopy, including Rothschild's slipper orchid (bottom right) which grows in Borneo's rain forests. In turn, these attract insects such as this orchid bee (bottom left) snapped visiting a Stanhopea *hanging-basket orchid in Costa Rica.*

Butterflies do their courting above the canopy. Large male morpho butterflies gather here to attract females, and can be seen by bush pilots flying over the forest.

SPLASH OF COLOUR A dipterocarp flowers in the Danum Valley, Sabah, Borneo. Flowering here usually occurs every five years or so, when cool, dry air arrives from Thailand's Khorat Plateau and the temperature drops.

TOWERING ABOVE THE CANOPY ARE THE GIANTS OF THE RAIN FOREST, A SCATTERING OF VERY TALL TREES KNOWN AS 'EMERGENTS'. They tower 60 m or more above the ground and their crowns are up to 30 m across. Situated up above the canopy, the crowns of these trees are exposed to stronger, drier winds and their leaves tend to be waxy to limit water loss. In the Amazon, the tallest tree is the silk cotton, or kapok, tree. It has a large trunk, up to 5 m in circumference, and huge buttress roots. A spreading fan of shallow true roots support its base. Its branches are covered with simple thorns and it sheds its palm-like leaves in the dry season. Its flowers, which bloom before the new growth of leaves, have an unpleasant smell that attracts bats. The silk cotton gets its name from the fibrous lining of its seedpods, a material that cannot be spun, like cotton, but is used to fill pillows and mattresses. Although originating in South America, it also grows in rain forests elsewhere in the world.

In South-east Asia, the tallest canopy trees are dipterocarps. This family of 515 species dominates the rain forests there. A few species are found in Africa, and just one in South America. Dipterocarps tend to flower after periods of particularly heavy rain,

OVERSTOREY

BOMBERS AND EXPLOSIVES

Just as butterflies, birds and bats can move about freely above the canopy, so emergent trees produce seeds designed to fly, too. Wind dispersal is a popular method of seed dispersal, as it requires little energy for maximum effect. The plant world's most perfectly designed flying seed must be that of the Asian climbing gourd (left), found in the tropical forests of the Sunda Islands in the Malay Archipelago. Its football-sized gourds are packed with hundreds of winged seeds (above), which drop into the air, like squadrons of stealth bombers. Their papery, membranous wings are 13 cm across, and they glide gently in wide circles through the forest canopy. Since seeds are vulnerable to seed predators, trees tend to disperse their seeds in one explosive event, known as 'mass seeding'. In the Congo, the pods of the oil bean tree explode with such force the seeds are flung more than 30 m from the tree. The sound is said to send forest elephants fleeing in fright.

and all species flower within the same two-month period, bringing patches of vivid colour to the otherwise uniform rain-forest green.

Like all dipterocarps, the Philippine mahogany – one of the tallest trees in the Philippines – relies on the tiniest of insects in order to reproduce. The tree's flowers do not produce nectar, which would lure in bees, beetles and moths. Instead, they emit a perfume that attracts swarms of thrips, or thunderflies. These minute insects, no more than 1 mm long with feathery wings, chew at the flowers and pollen – but they are more than rain-forest scroungers. Before morning, the chewed flowers drop from the tree, carrying the pollen-covered thrips to the ground. As the air warms in the daytime, the thrips drift back up to the canopy where they are attracted to new flowers and pollinate them.

Colourful characters

The emergent trees are where many of the larger rain-forest birds reside. The tops of these statuesque trees are the preferred nesting sites for birds of prey, such as the harpy eagle. At this height the nests are safe from predators and the adult birds have a clear view of any prey in the surrounding forest. The largest of the parrots – the brightly coloured macaws – also like to make use of the tall trees. In South and Central America, there are about 16 known macaw species, all with hooked bills that they use to break into hard fruits and even nuts. Their feet have two toes pointing forwards and two pointing backwards, enabling the macaw to grasp branches firmly and to pick up food items and lift them to its mouth. Its tail is as long as its body and its wings are tapered for fast flight. Macaws nest in hollows in the trees.

Butterflies do their courting above the canopy. Large male morpho butterflies gather up here to attract the females, and are clearly visible from bush planes flying over the forest. Morpho butterflies need to act quickly because the insect's entire life cycle lasts just three months, the adults living for less than a month. Scientists developing anti-counterfeiting technology for currency and credit cards are studying the optical properties of the iridescent blue of the blue morpho's wings.

RAIN-FOREST CAVES

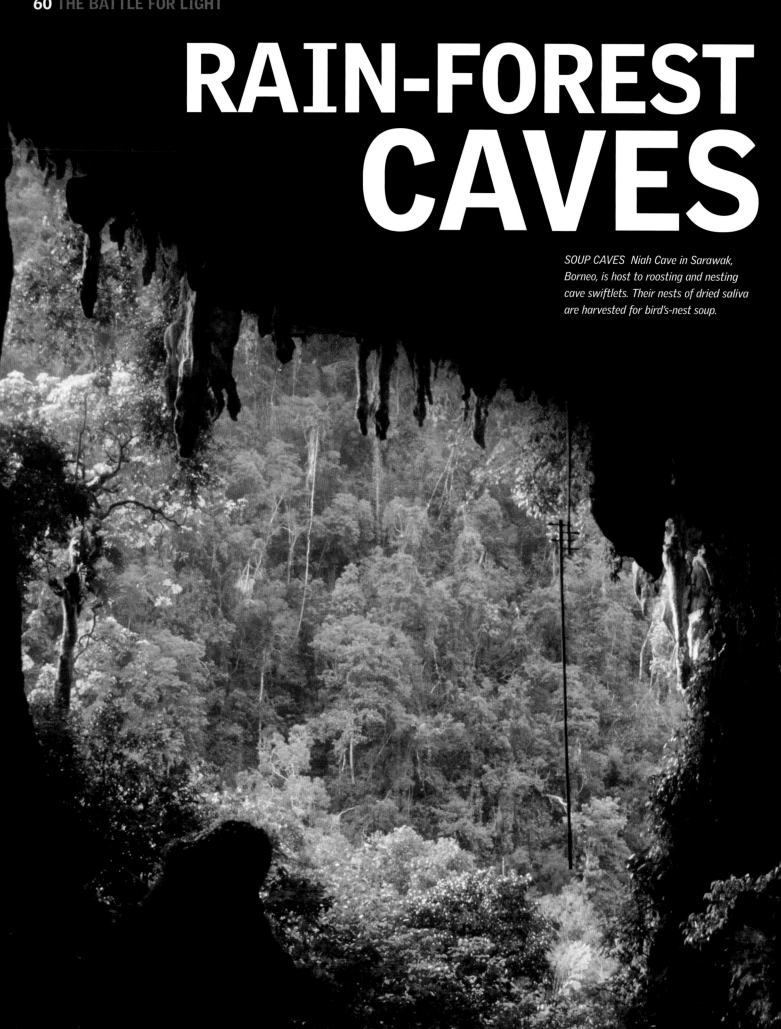

SOUP CAVES Niah Cave in Sarawak, Borneo, is host to roosting and nesting cave swiftlets. Their nests of dried saliva are harvested for bird's-nest soup.

DARK AND HIDDEN WORLDS EXIST IN THE HEARTS OF SOME RAIN FORESTS, IN THE CAVES THAT HAVE BEEN CARVED OUT OVER THE CENTURIES BY FOREST STREAMS. Some caverns are vast – up to 90 m high and equally wide, resembling natural cathedrals in the depths of the forest. The caves support complex ecosystems that rely on the comings and goings of birds and bats, which feed in the forest and roost in the caves. Their droppings provide food for an entire community of cave residents.

Cave communities

Deep in the forests of Sarawak, on the island of Borneo, some of the world's largest caves are home to huge numbers of cave swiftlets and bats. The swiftlets construct shelf-like nests adhering to the cave walls. The nests of some species are made only of saliva, and these are the ones prized by collectors, who climb to the cave roof on spindly ladders made of bamboo and rope to collect the nests for bird's-nest soup, an oriental delicacy.

The swiftlets stream out of the cave at dawn to feed on insects in the forests. As they do so, they meet bats returning from their night's hunting, and the shift change does not go unnoticed. Bat hawks patrol the area at dawn and dusk, swooping on the birds and bats as they negotiate the cave entrances. The bats leave the caves between five o'clock and seven in the evening, the sinuous cloud of 1.8 million free-tail and wrinkle-lipped bats pouring from the cave entrance like waves of thick, black smoke as they head off to hunt night-flying insects. The bats from one cave may catch 10–20 tonnes of insects each night.

Inside the caves, small mountains of bat and bird guano accumulate. In some caves the guano slopes are covered with a seething mass of golden cockroaches; in other caves, earwigs or

BAT CATCHER The Cuban boa wraps itself around a branch and catches bats as they fly in and out of their roosting caves. It locates them by detecting the heat of their bodies and their movement through the air.

crickets dominate. Long-legged cave spiders and centipedes prey on the insects, and cave crabs wallow in the guano streams, busily sifting out edible particles from the sediment. Snakes hanging from stalactites in the narrower passageways reach out and grab bats or swiftlets from mid-air, detecting the warmth of their bodies or the shockwaves they cause as they fly through the air. Sambar deer and bearded pigs from the forest sometimes enter the caves to eat the guano, which provides a mineral supplement to make up for deficiencies in their diet.

ANIMAL
POWER

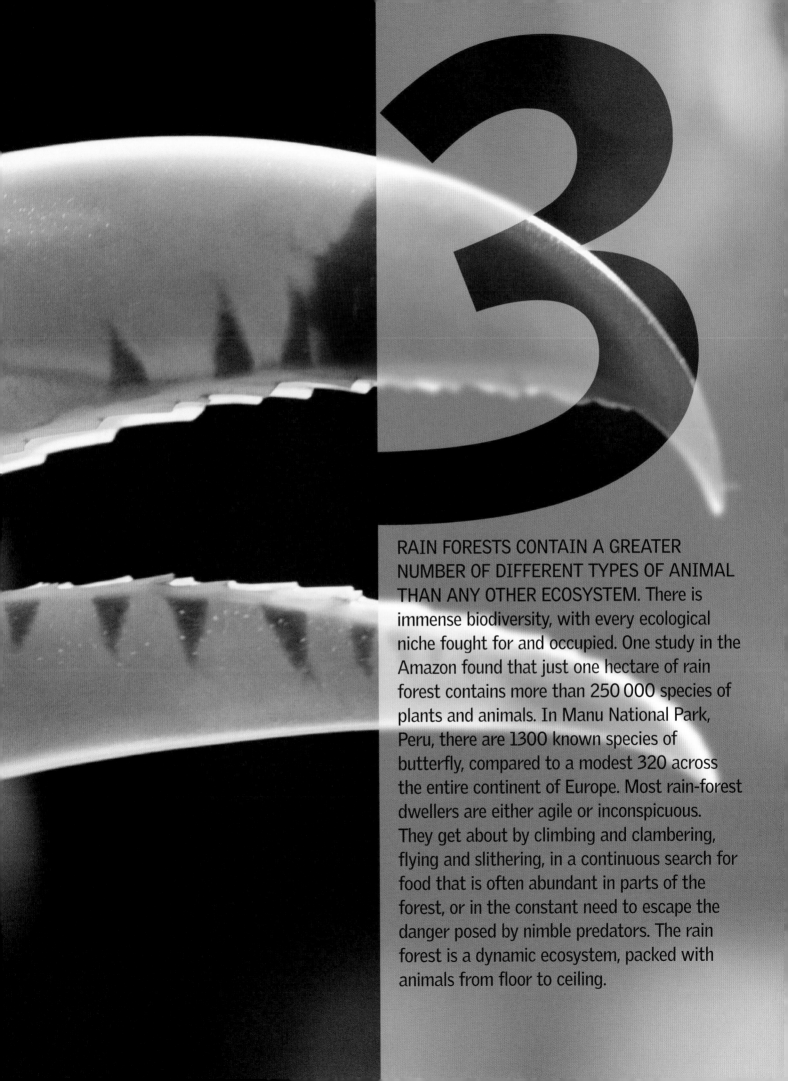

3

RAIN FORESTS CONTAIN A GREATER NUMBER OF DIFFERENT TYPES OF ANIMAL THAN ANY OTHER ECOSYSTEM. There is immense biodiversity, with every ecological niche fought for and occupied. One study in the Amazon found that just one hectare of rain forest contains more than 250 000 species of plants and animals. In Manu National Park, Peru, there are 1300 known species of butterfly, compared to a modest 320 across the entire continent of Europe. Most rain-forest dwellers are either agile or inconspicuous. They get about by climbing and clambering, flying and slithering, in a continuous search for food that is often abundant in parts of the forest, or in the constant need to escape the danger posed by nimble predators. The rain forest is a dynamic ecosystem, packed with animals from floor to ceiling.

HANGING BY A TAIL

CREATURES THAT LIVE HIGH IN THE CANOPY FACE THE CONSTANT CHALLENGE OF NEGOTIATING GAPS BETWEEN TREES AND BRANCHES AS THEY MOVE ABOUT IN SEARCH OF FOOD. In response, some have become expert climbers, and some of these have developed an additional safety feature – a grasping, or prehensile, tail. This is predominantly, but not exclusively, a New World adaptation, found mainly among mammals. The South American forests are denser than those of other continents, with more lianas and vines, which favour climbing as a way of getting about.

Many New World monkeys, including howler and spider monkeys, have prehensile tails that can support the animal's entire weight as it climbs through the trees or dangles to reach food at the ends of thin branches. The tails of these species have a bare tactile pad at the tip for an improved grip, and the monkeys can also use them to

CURLY TAIL *The spotted cuscus is one of the few marsupials of Australia and New Guinea to have a prehensile tail. Its tail has rasp-like scales on the bare underside which helps it to grasp branches.*

LENDING A HAND Woolly spider monkeys in
Brazil's Atlantic coast forests use their prehensile
tails to hang from branches, freeing up their hands
to reach for the young leaves and ripe fruits that
make up the bulk of their diet.

hold and manipulate objects such as food. In the Amazon's
old-growth, or terra-firma, forest, woolly spider monkeys are
rather timid, and at the slightest hint of danger they move
rapidly away through the topmost branches of the canopy,
travelling in line abreast like a weather front sweeping across
the forest, using their prehensile tails to ensure they do not fall.
When undisturbed, they feed on fruit from more than 200 tree
species and drink from bromeliad pools. They are often followed
by toucans, which depend on the monkeys' alertness for signs
of danger, and by forest hawks, which grab insects disturbed by
the monkeys as they crash through the trees.

Although most mammals with fully prehensile tails are
monkeys, several non-primates use their tails in the same way.
The nocturnal kinkajou, or honey bear, of Central and South
America uses its grasping tail to climb through the trees, but not
to hold onto food like monkeys sometimes do. The binturong, or
Asian bearcat, of Borneo is neither bear nor cat, but one of the
civet-genet family, and it, too, uses its tail for climbing. It has
another useful adaptation: it can rotate its back legs in order to
retain its grip when descending a tree head first.

Marsupial climbers

Several species of marsupial have prehensile tails, including the
cuscus family, nocturnal inhabitants of tropical rain forests in
South-east Asia and Australasia. Some, such as the Sulawesi

cuscus, are the size of mice, while others, such as the common
spotted cuscus, are the size of a large house cat. The spotted
cuscus sleeps in tree hollows during the day, but at night it
forages for fruits and young leaves, and is partial to birds' eggs if
it can find them. With its big forward-facing eyes, the spotted
cuscus was thought at first to be a monkey, although its slow,
deliberate movements are more reminiscent of a sloth. When in
danger it barks a warning and slashes out with its front claws.

Partially prehensile tails

Capuchin monkeys of South America do not have a bare patch on
their tails, so they cannot grip food with them, but they are able
to use their tails to climb trees and dangle from branches. Tree
porcupines, silky anteaters, tamanduas and the marsupial Monito
del Monte of the New World also all have a tail they can use for
climbing. In the Old World, the only seriously prehensile tail is
sported by the tree pangolin, or scaly anteater, of African rain
forests. It even has the bare patch that some monkeys have, and
sometimes hangs by its tail while breaking into arboreal termite
nests, consuming up to 200 g of insects in a night.

A few reptiles and amphibians have grasping tails.
Chameleons in Madagascan rain forests can use their tails to
steady themselves when moving hesitatingly through the canopy.
The aptly named prehensile-tailed skink, a lizard that lives in
forests on the Solomon Islands archipelago, can move its tail in
just about any direction and curl it around branches for balance.
The crested gecko from New Caledonia has 'sticky' pads on the
base of its feet and a prehensile tail with a flattened tip, and can
climb just about any vertical surface. In Central America,
members of the web-footed salamander family use a prehensile
tail when clambering up moss-encrusted treetrunks and branches.

Pygmy anomalures, or flying mice, are no bigger than house mice, yet they can glide up to 50 m from one tree to the next.

LONG-DISTANCE GLIDER
The sugar glider's flying membranes extend from the fifth finger of the forelimb to the first toe on the hind limb, and enable this flying possum to glide for 50 m or more.

UNEXPECTED AVIATORS

THE RAIN FORESTS OF SOUTH-EAST ASIA ARE HOME TO SEVERAL REPTILE AND MAMMAL SPECIES, WHICH HAVE EVOLVED ADAPTATIONS THAT ENABLE THEM TO FLY, OR AT LEAST TO GLIDE, FROM TREE TO TREE. Asian rain forests are more open than those of South America and they lack extensive systems of vines and understorey vegetation connecting adjacent trees. If the gap between trees is too great to leap, an animal must climb down to the ground, where it is at risk from predators. Gliding is a much safer alternative.

Gliding *Draco* lizards are South-east Asia's most skilled flying reptiles. Their wings are formed from membrane between the ribs, which are detached at one end. The lizard uses the muscles in its chest, which in other animals lift the ribcage during breathing, to pull the ribs forward and outwards, creating a wing on either side of its body. The wings do not flap up and down, but provide sufficient lift for the lizard to make an extended glide from the treetops with a little in-flight manoeuvrability.

Some lizards have more flying power than others. The black-bearded gliding lizard has a thin neck, bulbous head and large wings. It attains lift immediately on take-off, even at relatively slow speeds, and can steer well in mid air. The orange-bearded gliding lizard has a robust body and small wings. When it jumps from the tree, it plummets down with its wings folded until it picks up enough speed to open them and glide. Of necessity, it lives at the top of the tallest trees in the forest.

Geckos are more usually associated with the ability to climb smooth surfaces, even glass, but some species can fly. Their wings, when not in use, are no more than flaps of skin rolled against the belly, but these flaps balloon out when the lizard starts its glide. Flaps at the side of the head, neck, tail and the rear edge of the hind limbs, together with webbing on the toes, enhance its gliding efficiency. The overall effect is more like a parachute than a glider, but even so Kuhl's flying gecko can change direction by 180 degrees during flight.

Flying snakes and frogs

Peninsular Malaysia has three species of tree snake that have evolved the ability to glide. The snake flings itself into space by forming a J-shape with its body. During flight it flattens and widens its body like a parasail and wriggles in a way that is analogous to a Frisbee, giving it stabilised flight.

Giant webbed hands and feet are the airfoils used by Wallace's flying frog and the Harlequin flying frog. These frogs can steer and make sharp turns in mid-air, reaching their breeding sites on the ground in super-quick time.

Forest gliders

Queensland in Australia and New Guinea are home to marsupial gliders, such as the sugar and mahogany gliders. Flaps of skin stretched between the fore and hind legs on either side of the

AIRBORNE FROG Wallace's gliding frog is actually a parachutist. It drifts down through the canopy using the enlarged webbing between its toes as parachutes. It can travel for about 15 m to a neighbouring tree.

body allow them to glide for up to 50 m. They use their tails to stabilise their bodies during flight. Mahogany gliders are longer than sugar gliders, and they do their gliding at night in the constant search for nectar, pollen and the gum that seeps from wounds in trees. They also eat spiders and insects, but they have to watch their backs lest they fall prey to rufous and sooty owls.

The canopy in African rain forests has breaks, and the anomalures, or scaly squirrels, have bridged the gap by gliding. They have two rods of cartilage, like the spokes of an umbrella, sticking out on either side of the body, and these support membranes stretching between the fore and hind legs. On the underside of the tail are scales (hence the creature's common name) that help them grip the landing site. They can travel as far as 100 m in a single glide. Pygmy anomalures, or flying mice, are no bigger than house mice, yet they can glide up to 50 m from one tree to the next.

STREAMLINED LIZARD In addition to wings, the Draco gliding lizard has flaps on either side of its neck that act as stabilisers, and hind limbs with a cross-section similar to an aircraft's wing.

FOREST OF
THE APES

THE VAST RAIN FOREST OF THE CONGO BASIN IN CENTRAL
AFRICA IS HOME TO THREE SPECIES OF HIGHER APES –
BONOBOS, CHIMPANZEES AND LOWLAND GORILLAS.
These are humankind's nearest relatives, which begs the
question: could our origins be in the tropical rain forest along
with our close relatives, rather than on the open plains of the
savannah? It is a conundrum with which scientists studying early humans still
grapple. There is evidence to suggest that early humans – the so-called 'ape-men' –
were prey for the crowned hawk eagle, a rain-forest predator that snatched baby
ape-men from the forest floor, just as eagles catch monkeys today.

FORMIDABLE GROUP *Lowland rain
forests are often flooded, so ground-
living animals must be able to cope
with water. Common chimpanzees do
not swim, but will walk upright like us
to wade through water.*

Bloodthirsty apes

The great Congo River flows through the heart of the region, and the area to its north is home to the rain-forest's chimpanzees. Common chimpanzees are the most aggressive apes. They hunt monkeys, such as the colobus, for their meat, and kill and sometimes eat others of their own kind in wars between groups. They also indulge in infanticide. They will kill leopard cubs, the offspring of their number-one natural enemy, and they have also been known to kill human infants.

Chimpanzees are strong, with a pull five to six times stronger than a human's. They are also the most inventive of the great apes as they use tools, a behaviour once thought to be exclusive to humans but which is now known to be more widespread in the animal kingdom. They use stones to crack nuts, and sticks to fish for termites and angle for driver ants. Adult chimps in Senegal have even been seen to take sticks and sharpen one end using their teeth to fashion spears, which they use to catch bushbabies asleep in the hollows of trees.

Chimpanzees eat a wide variety of plant food and do most of their feeding in the trees. They also construct sleeping nests in the trees each night. They tend to travel through the forest in small bands of about a dozen individuals, but these troops can get together to form groups up to 150 strong. If a troop comes across potential enemies, such as a leopard, members scream loudly and grab anything, such as sticks and stones, that they can hurl at the threat. Nevertheless, chimpanzees often succumb to leopard predation, especially when caught unawares in their sleeping nests at night.

Lion killers

A population of large, black-faced apes, resembling giant chimpanzees, has been discovered in the northerly Bili-Bondo region of the northern Congo rain forest. Rather than fleeing, as most chimpanzees would do, they approach and even attack any human intruders. They have no fear, an attribute that may be unique in all of Africa. They are larger than normal chimpanzees, up to 2 m tall, and twice the weight of common chimpanzees, according to local reports. They might well represent a new species or subspecies of chimpanzee, but they behave more like gorillas, nesting on the ground and rarely climbing into the trees. It is thought that the large males retire at night to the ground nests, while the females and juveniles sleep in tree nests. They peel bananas using their hands rather than their teeth, and the tools they use to 'fish' for termites are over a metre long – much larger than those used by other chimpanzees. Local people call them the 'lion killers', in contrast to the 'tree beaters' – their name for common chimps in the area. The lion killers move about the forest and hunt in silence.

Few scientists have come face to face with these apes, but they have found well-worn ground nests and droppings, analysis of which indicates an animal that eats fruit, a trait of chimpanzees rather than gorillas. Their footprints are much larger than those of chimps or even gorillas, and the females lack the genital swelling of female chimps. On moonlit nights, especially with a full moon, they howl like wolves. The danger now is that poachers will kill these unusually large apes. The area is essentially lawless, and the apes do not live in a reserve. They are truly wild animals, but they could disappear before anybody has a chance to study them closely.

Love, not war

On the south side of the Congo River, keeping well away from their more hostile common chimpanzee relatives, live bonobos, or pygmy chimpanzees, the pacifists of the ape world. Bonobos use sexual contact, in same-sex and opposite-sex interactions, and even between parent and offspring, for greetings, bonding and maintaining harmony within the group. This taboo-breaking approach suggests that sexual contact is an important behaviour in bonobo society, used to de-fuse stressful situations and conflict. Instead of fighting or fleeing, bonobos use sex.

Bonobos walk upright about 25 per cent of the time, and have distinct facial differences from each other, which aids recognition between individuals. Although vocal calls are the main form of communication, facial expressions are also important, especially in indicating different moods, such as relaxedness, playfulness or aggression. When members of the group come across a new source of food, they utter feeding calls and point to indicate where the food can be found.

ALMOST HUMAN A group of bonobos, or pygmy chimpanzees, gather food much like we would. Genetically, they are little different from us, and by watching bonobos it is not hard to see how our ancient ancestors might have behaved millions of years ago.

RAIN-FOREST LOVERS In bonobo society mating is used to reduce tension and release aggression. Bonobos are unusual among primates in that they mate in many different positions, including belly-to-belly.

Males are a little larger than females. Unlike the males of other great apes, they help with the family. Although females do most of the work involved in raising the young, a father will comfort a youngster who is hurt and will even carry offspring on his back. A female starts reproducing at about 12 years of age, and will have one baby every five to six years. She has a menstrual cycle of roughly 49 days, and she is fertile for about 75 per cent of the time.

Bonobos live in groups containing both males and females. Should a group become too large, a few members will split off and either form a new group or amalgamate with a smaller neighbouring group. The family is at the core of bonobo society, and individuals rarely live alone. Females tend to rule the roost, although rank appears to be less important to bonobos than in other primate societies.

A group will occupy an area of forest about 20 km wide, and although this might overlap with the home ranges of other groups, bonobos rarely come to blows. If food is scarce, a large group might chase off a smaller one, otherwise they avoid each other's company. Groups forage during the day, sometimes breaking into smaller foraging parties; the distance travelled depends on the abundance of food. Bonobos are mainly vegetarian, eating mostly fruit, but if this is in short supply they will feed on shoots, leaves, flowers and herbs – in all, they eat about 133 different species of plant. They eat meat occasionally, with insects, flying squirrels and the occasional baby duiker, a small forest antelope, turning up on the menu. Essential minerals are obtained by eating termite clay.

At dusk, the foraging parties reconvene and members clamber into the trees to build night nests. Bonobos have few enemies, save the leopard, which hunts them at night, and humans, who kill them for bushmeat.

King of the forest

Gorillas are the largest primates. The biggest males weigh up to 225 kg and stand nearly 1.8 m tall. Females are half their size. Of the two main species – the lowland and mountain gorillas – it is the lowland gorilla that occupies the Congo rain forest. It is less hairy than its mountain cousin, and is considerably shyer. Small groups of 5 to 25 individuals, consisting of a silverback – the dominant male recognised by the grey hair on his back – and several juveniles and mothers with babies, are seen most often in clearings, alongside forest elephants and antelope, where they

forage for tubers. They are mainly vegetarian, but like chimpanzees they supplement their diet with ants and termites and with minerals from soil.

Gorillas also 'wadge' their food. They sandwich fresh or overripe fruit between leaves in their mouth and squeeze out the juice – a natural gorilla smoothie. In this way, they avoid swallowing poisonous seeds or eating too much fibre. They may suck on the wadge for ten minutes or more, spitting it out when they have finished. There is also some evidence for tool use. A female was once seen to use a stick to check the depth of water before crossing a stream, and one individual has been seen breaking open palm nuts using a rock. This means that all the African great apes have been seen to use tools.

Natural ape medicines

Gorillas, chimps and bonobos regularly eat medicinal plants, especially the bitter-tasting *ngoka*, which is found along streams in swampy areas, a species of woody vine known as *kusa*, and the leaves of Vernonia, an ironweed, and Aspilia, a wild creeping sunflower. Chimpanzees do not stuff Aspilia leaves into their mouths, as they do other food, but carefully roll the leaves between the tongue and the roof of the mouth and swallow them whole. The Aspilia leaves contain a powerful antibiotic that is effective against parasites.

Gorillas chew only the tips of *ngoka* leaves. Normally they would eat an entire leaf, so this indicates to watching scientists that nibbling *ngoka* leaves is probably a form of self-medication. Further evidence for this comes from local people, who use the same plant to treat diarrhoea, colic and fevers, and as a purge to get rid of internal parasites, such as tapeworms. They also use the leaf sap as eyewash, and put crumpled leaves on wounds – evidence that the rain forests contain much that would benefit humans.

SIGNALLING

DAWN IN THE RAIN FOREST IS GREETED BY SOME OF THE MOST HAUNTING SOUNDS IN NATURE. In South and Central America, howler monkeys deliver a chorus; gibbons in South-east Asia and indris in Madagascar sing duets. The songs and calls are a way to overcome a communications problem – how to get your message through the forest when laying claim to a territory or warning neighbours not to invade your patch. Visual signals are not a long-range option because of the dense vegetation, so some primates sing or call like birds.

In the Amazon and in rain forests in Central America, howler monkeys call every morning with a surprisingly loud growling chorus. The sounds can be heard from 5 km or more across the forest, making them the world's loudest monkey and possibly the loudest land animal. The sound is made by passing air over a cavity in a large bone – the hyoid – in the monkey's throat. Males produce a deep roaring sound, while females grunt. They live in groups of up to 30 individuals, and the chorus at dawn and again at dusk is the means by which a troop ensures that its neighbours are not too close, limiting fights

BIG EYES The owl butterfly startles any predator by opening its wings and showing the large eye-spots on their upper surfaces. It is a form of inter-species communication, with the butterfly saying 'I'm much bigger than you'.

between troops. The howler is one of the New World's largest monkeys and it is a slow mover, using its tail like a fifth limb to grab hold of branches as it travels through the canopy. It feeds mainly on leaves, the area within which it forages being a moving territory rather than a fixed patch of forest.

In South-east Asia, male and female gibbons join voices in a haunting duet that echoes through the rain forest first thing in the morning. Pairs of gibbons proclaim the right to their territory, each of the 12 known species with its own identifiable song. The silvery or moloch gibbon on the island of Java is the exception. The female sings a solo, the male contributing little or nothing to the performance. At first light, he watches for danger while she delivers her haunting song. Often her song is combined with bursts of jumping about in the canopy and swinging from branches. Then she, her mate and her offspring go foraging in the forest for the fruit on which they feed. Gibbons also sing a song, quite different to the morning territorial duet, that is specific to an intruding predator. Like a jungle telegraph, the threat song is passed from one group to the next so all the gibbons in the forest are alert to the danger.

The tamarins of South America's rain forests make sounds more reminiscent of birds than monkeys. The cotton-topped tamarin, for example, emits whistles,

quiet chirping sounds and high-pitched trills in a vocabulary of 38 recognised sounds. The sounds also have grammatical rules, enabling these tiny New World monkeys to express fear, curiosity and playfulness. They have calls that warn of danger and special sounds given to youngsters.

There are no less than eight types of chirping, from sounds emitted when mobbing a predator to those given to familiar objects. Squeals are intensified into twitters and chatters if an animal is frightened, trills are made to infants and whistles accompany grooming. Tamarins announce their presence with a long, loud territorial call, and anger or inquisitiveness is accompanied by 'tonguing' – the tamarin moves its tongue rapidly in and out across its lips. A serious threat from another tamarin is greeted with silence. The little monkey furrows its brow until the skin almost covers its eyes, pouts its lips and raises the fur on its neck and head.

Listening in

Many species of rain-forest monkeys, lemurs and other noisy mammals not only listen to the calls of their own species, but also recognise the warning yelps, screeches, screams and squawks of other species in order to pick up an early warning of approaching danger. This cross-species communication is not confined to mammals. In West Africa, yellow-casqued hornbills pay close attention to the warning calls of Diana monkeys, the troop of monkeys and the flock of birds foraging alongside each other in the treetops. The monkeys have distinct alarm calls for specific predators, a predator on the ground, such as a leopard, prompting a different cry to a monkey-eating eagle flying

MORNING CALLER Howler monkeys from Central and South America greet the dawn with a loud, roaring call. Neighbouring troops sometimes approach to within feet of each other and begin a deafening roaring fight.

NIGHT CALLER The male masked mud puddle frog inflates its vocal sacs and lets rip with a piercing 'whine-chuck-chuck' call. He uses his voice to impress females, but it can also attract a bat that homes in on the call to catch a meal.

A predator relies mainly on stealth in order to snatch a monkey or a bird from the trees, so the louder hornbill calls signal to the predator that it has been spotted, robbing it of the element of surprise.

Visual attraction

The rain forest is not an ideal place for visual signalling because the branches and leaves get in the way, yet some creatures have adopted visual means to attract a mate or warn off rivals and predators. Male birds often display bright colours, or have elaborate feathers or bill to impress females. Bright yellow and red signals show up in the understorey where the main colour is brown; blue and ultraviolet signals (some birds see in ultraviolet) are conspicuous in the canopy, where green predominates. In Australia and New Guinea, for example, male brush turkeys, or megapodes, have colourful heads, necks and headcombs that are more brightly coloured during the breeding season. Lizards, such as anole lizards, nod their head or flash a colourful flap of skin under the chin, called the dewlap, and the more busy the background of leaves and branches, the more vigorous the signalling.

overhead. Monkeys and hornbills both fall prey to crowned eagles, but leopards are only interested in monkeys and not birds. If a monkey spots a crowned eagle, it gives the alarm call and the entire flock of hornbills joins in the chorus. All are on full alert. If the predator is a leopard, the birds, who can distinguish between the two calls, ignore the leopard alarm call.

The monkeys also gain something from the arrangement. Their calls penetrate no more than 500 m through the forest, while the hornbill calls carry for up to 2 km, so the hornbill calls are more likely to be heard by the predator.

Butterflies and moths often use a form of mimicry to warn off predators. They have huge eye-spots on their wings. When the wings are opened, the predator is startled by what looks like a giant face. Eye-spots on the elaborate tail displays of birds such as South-east Asia's Argus and Palawan pheasants are there to catch the attention of the opposite sex. The more eye-spots, the more likely the male is to attract a partner.

Not all colour signals take place between animals. Flowers have colours and patterns that attract insects and other potential pollinators. On the island of Mauritius, local geckos are attracted more to plants that colour their nectar than to those that do not. The coloured, rather than the more usually clear, nectar is thought to be an 'honesty' signal, enabling potential pollinators to gauge how much nectar the plant really has before visiting. Some plants signal to animals that their fruit is ready to be picked by changing its colour from dull greens or browns to bright reds and oranges. In this way, the plant recruits animals to help spread its seeds.

MANDRILL

THE WORLD'S MOST COLOURFUL, POWERFUL

AND AGGRESSIVE MONKEYS ARE THE MANDRILLS, OR MAN-APES, WHICH LIVE IN THE RAIN FORESTS OF CENTRAL AFRICA. They form some of the largest known primate groups – troops of more than 1000 animals have been seen – and they sweep through the forest, making contact calls of barks, grunts, squeals and screams as they go. They also communicate visually. Although in the gloom of the forest floor, their olive coats blend in with the greens and browns around them, their brightly coloured faces are highly visible, the blue ridges sported by both sexes resembling a snarl and the red stripes on the males indicating dominance. Bright colours on the rump also help members of the group to keep in contact. The colours intensify when an individual is more excited; the blue on the buttocks and chest become brighter, and red spots appear on wrists and ankles.

VITAL STATISTICS

CLASS: Mammalia
ORDER: Primates
SPECIES: *Mandrillus sphinx*
HABITAT: Dense rain forest
DISTRIBUTION: Congo, Gabon, Guinea and Cameroon
DIET: Fruit, leaves, roots and insects
KEY FEATURE: Brightly coloured beards, snouts and rumps.

EXTRAVAGANT BIRDS

SOME OF THE MOST EXTRAVAGANT COURTSHIP DISPLAYS IN THE ANIMAL WORLD ARE PERFORMED BY RAIN-FOREST DWELLERS, who must catch the attention of potential suitors while avoiding being spotted by a predator.

In many species it is the female's prerogative to choose a partner, and the males have to demonstrate their prowess. Birds have taken this aspect of signalling to an extreme, some species going in for short bursts of attention-grabbing activity, while others rely on exotic plumage.

Lords of the dance

Many rain-forest birds perform a dance to attract a mate, but the manakins of South and Central America have developed this into an art form. In the Amazon, male swallow-tailed manakins perform the 'catherine-wheel dance', or 'jump display', in groups of three at display sites, or leks. When a female appears, the three approach her. The first male leaps into the air and then flies backwards to the back of the queue. The second male performs the same dance, and then the third. They continue until the female chooses the best performer, usually the dominant member of the trio.

MOONWALKING MANAKIN The red-capped manakin displays in the canopy. When a female arrives he performs a dance with snapping wings and buzzing calls. If the female likes what she sees, he flies into the upper canopy and then dive-bombs and screams at her.

BIG PERFORMANCE The male cock-of-the-rocks of South America puts on a raucous display in an arena on the forest floor, or around mossy branches.

Elsewhere in the Amazon rain forest, a second male wire-tailed manakin joins a dominant male, and together they dance to entice females closer. The dominant bird then tickles the female under the chin with special wire-like feathers in his tail.

The bright orange or red cock-of-the-rocks is another impressive dancer. Two species are found in South American rain forests. In the misty dawn, males wait for females to visit the lek. If a female ventures close, 20–30 males may swoop in and compete for the right to occupy the best sites. When the female comes closer, the males erupt in a dramatic show of screams, wing-flashing and head-cocking. They strut, bow, jump, snap their bills and call loudly. If the female is unimpressed she leaves, and the lek falls silent until another female appears. When the Sun comes up the males disperse, as female cock-of-the-rocks are not the only creatures attracted by the rowdy performance. Eagles, ocelots and jaguars would not turn up their noses at these tasty titbits. And during their displays, the males are so wrapped up in their dance that they are oblivious to approaching predators.

Putting on a show

In South-east Asia and in Queensland, Australia, female birds of paradise are cryptic, blending in with their rain-forest habitat, but the males are brightly coloured and very overstated, with prominent feathers on their heads, tails or wings. The males of many bird of paradise species strut at a lek, while others have elaborate courtship dances. They do little but eat, display and, if they are lucky, mate. One of the most colourful is Wilson's bird-

DANCING IN THE DARK The male Wilson's bird of paradise clears a patch of forest floor on which to perform. The blue patch of skin on the back of the head is clearly visible even in the dark forest.

FOREST-BUILDER Using two branches as supports, the male golden bowerbird constructs a two-tower, maypole-type bower out of twigs in order to impress females. The maypoles are about 2 m high, and are decorated with flowers and lichens.

of-paradise, found only on Batanta and Waigeo islands off the western tip of New Guinea. The crown on the top of its head glows neon blue, complementing its green, gold and red plumage as its dances around its display area.

On the main island, the exceedingly rare male blue bird-of-paradise performs its display hanging upside down from a branch. Halmahera Island in Indonesia is home to Wallace's standardwing, the males of which display in a lekking tree. Only the males occupying the best sites attract females, and they must also have the most impressive, long, white plumes trailing from their wings. The smaller sickletails have bright blue legs and feet, and include the magnificent bird-of-paradise, with its orange wings and sickle-like green tail feathers, and the king bird-of-paradise. The larger sickletails include the black sicklebird, with iridescent green, blue and purple feathers, long curved bill and sabre-shaped tail.

All the forest is a stage
Bowerbirds, which live in New Guinea and Queensland rain forests, do not adopt the colourful plumage of the birds-of-paradise – they are rather drab in comparison. Instead, the male bowerbird builds an elaborate structure of twigs, leaves and anything he can

BALLETIC DANCE The male western parotia, a bird-of-paradise from western New Guinea, shakes his head and neck vigorously during his display to show off the silver, shield-shaped adornment on the top of his head.

purloin to impress the females. There are 20 species, each constructing a different type of display area to attract a partner. The tooth-billed catbird builds a bower resembling a circus ring, while the golden bowerbird perches on a platform between two towers made from twigs. The satin bowerbird builds an avenue bower, much like a city street. Macgregor's bowerbird constructs a maypole, and the spotted bowerbird builds a wide straw wall and dances energetically in front of it.

Most bowerbirds decorate their bowers with objects they have collected, both natural and man-made – shells, leaves, flowers, stones, shards of glass and plastic objects. The satin bowerbird has a predilection for blue things, which have been seen to include blue shotgun shell cases, blue toothbrushes, clothes pegs and bottle tops. Several bowerbirds, including the regent bowerbird, paint the walls of their bower with plant juices. No two bowers are the same, and birds spend hours arranging their display. Everything has its place, and should an object move while the bird is away, it is put back in exactly the same place on its return. Birds also steal objects from their neighbours. Females inspect the structures on display, and select the male with the most striking bower.

COLOUR CHANGE

A FEW RAIN-FOREST ANIMALS CAN ACTUALLY CHANGE THEIR COLOUR. Some use colour changes to blend in with their surroundings and conceal themselves from predators or prey; others to give a warning. Some register their mood through changes in colour. Madagascar's rain forests are home to about half of the 135 species of chameleon to be found in Africa, southern Europe and parts of Asia. They are solitary lizards, and most are well adapted to life in the trees. They also change colour. It was once thought that chameleons adjusted their body colour to match their background, but their natural resting colour provides camouflage. The colour changes occur in response to mood, and sometimes to temperature or light.

In chameleons, colour changes can take place within minutes. Nerve or hormonal signals stimulate pigments to move in and out of special cells, known as chromatophores, below their transparent skin. Different combinations of pigment and light produce different colours. The outer chromatophores contain red or yellow pigments, and below these is a layer of colourless crystals that reflect white and blue light. If the upper layers of pigment show yellow, the combined effect with the reflected blue light is that the chameleon appears green – the mark of a 'calm'

In chameleons, colour changes can take place within minutes. In response to nerve or hormonal signals, pigments move in and out of special cells below their transparent skin.

TEMPERATURE SENSITIVE The higher the temperature and the lower the humidity, the more likely that White's tree frog of Australia and New Guinea is coloured a brighter blue-green.

chameleon. An agitated chameleon might appear more yellow as the yellow pigment cells expand and block the blue light. During the breeding season, male chameleons look spectacular in stripes and blotches of green, blue, yellow and brown. Females unwilling to mate announce their reticence by displaying red spots on their bodies. At night, when the chameleon is fully relaxed, it can become almost white. The fading colour seems to be linked to the animal closing its eyes. In the morning, when the air is cooler, it can appear darker in order to absorb more warmth from the Sun.

Deep in the Borneo rain forest lives the Kapuas mud snake. Discovered in 2003, it is a venomous, rear-fanged snake that grows to about 50 cm long. Its normal resting colour is reddish-brown with an iridescent sheen, but when scientists placed one in a bucket to take it back to camp, it turned white

BROWN IS COOL If the humidity is high and the temperature low, White's tree frog is more likely to be brown. Researchers think that the colour changes help the frog to control its body temperature as well as to blend in with its background.

within minutes. The rapid colour change could be a defence mechanism or a warning prior to striking out at an aggressor.

Many species of snake change colour. Rain-forest rattlesnakes can appear darker in the morning to absorb warmth. The green tree boa of Australian rain forests exhibits the most dramatic change. Young snakes, which are yellow or red, leave the rain forest and spend their first year in neighbouring grasslands, where they blend in with dried grass and fallen leaves. At about a year old they can take larger prey, so they move to the rain-forest canopy, where they hunt rodents and birds. Here, they slough off their yellow skin and adopt green as their adult colour.

Some frogs are capable of changing colour, usually in response to changes in the temperature of their surroundings: the cooler the weather or the water, the darker the frog. White's tree frog, which lives in the rain forests of Australia, New Guinea and some Indonesian islands, changes from green, grey or aqua-blue to brown. It is thought that they do this in response to environmental changes as well as for camouflage.

FOOD FOR

ALL

4

RAIN FORESTS OFFER ANIMALS A BROAD RANGE OF NUTRITIOUS FOODS. Whether giant trees, understorey ferns or clinging epiphytes, plants provide the energy that enables the forests' animal populations to survive and flourish. On the menu are nectar, pollen, flowers, leaves, gums and resins, fruits and nuts. Some animals – like this squirrel monkey tucking into a caterpillar – get extra nutrition by eating other creatures that feast on the forest bounty. In these most efficient of ecosystems, the plants benefit, too. In the process of taking food, animals often become the servants of the plants, helping them with pollination and seed dispersal. Animals are generally more reliable at carrying seeds and other reproductive products away from the parent plant than, say, wind or water. The result is that plants and animals have co-evolved to benefit from each other.

FLAPPING ITS WINGS AN AVERAGE OF 80 TIMES A SECOND, A HUMMINGBIRD CAN HOVER IN MID-AIR, FLY BACKWARDS AND EVEN VERTICALLY UP AND DOWN, MANOEUVRES FEW OTHER BIRDS CAN DO. Its heart can beat at an equally astounding 1260 times a minute. Just to exist a hummingbird needs to consume more than its own weight in food every day, and its chosen food is nectar. A hummingbird must visit hundreds of flowers every day to extract this high-energy, sugary solution. It has a long bill and an extendable, forked tongue with which to probe into flowers. It moves its wings so rapidly it does not need to perch on the lip of a flower; instead, it hovers in front of the flower as it feeds.

NECTAR-FEEDERS

The number of visits a hummingbird makes to flowers depends on the energy content of their sugars. A bird might make five visits in an hour to flowers with high-energy nectar, but 14 visits to those producing nectar with half the energy content. As a result, a hummingbird feeding on high-energy nectar collects more than five times its own weight of food in a day, while one feeding on lower-energy nectar collects 14 times its own weight. Nectar usually consists of three sugars – glucose, fructose and sucrose – with a small amount of protein, and sodium and potassium salts. Even so, a diet of pure nectar would result in nutritional deficiencies, so hummingbirds also catch small insects as part of their day's toil.

Hummingbirds are exclusive to the New World, but there are small birds in the Old World and in Australia that behave in a similar way. In African forests there are sunbirds and in Australia honeyeaters, both nectar feeders, and the smaller species are able to hover. The three bird groups are unrelated – they have evolved the same anatomy and behaviour quite separately on different continents, a phenomenon known as convergent evolution.

The plants these birds visit tend to have red or orange flowers, a sign of strengthened flower stalks to withstand the thrusting bills of hovering birds, or the weight of those that perch while they are feeding. Other, less robust flowers attract day-flying

FLASH OF BRILLIANCE A violet-fronted brilliant, a species of hummingbird, hovers in mid-air to extract nectar from dangling flowers in the Manu Cloud Forest of Peru.

A hummingbird feeding on high-energy nectar collects more than five times its own weight of food in a day; one feeding on lower-energy nectar collects up to 14 times its own weight.

forests. It uses this to reach the nectar at the bottom of the 30 cm deep comet orchid.

Night pollinators are attracted by night-blooming flowers, which grow on tree-trunks rather than branches. Many night-blooming flowers have large white petals that are visible in the forest gloom. Leaving nothing to chance, these plants also produce a musky scent that attracts another unexpected type of pollinator – bats. Nectar-feeding bats are important pollinators of tropical rain-forest plants. Like the larger fruit-eating bats, they rely on sight and a sophisticated sense of smell to locate nectar. They have a long, slender tongue that reaches deep inside a flower, and like the day-flying hummingbirds they need a good supply of their energy-drink. Bats burn sugar faster than any other mammal, as much as three times more than a top-flight athlete. Like the sphinx moth and the hummingbird, many species of nectar-feeding bats can hover.

nectar-feeding butterflies, such as the giant birdwing butterflies of South-east Asia and Australia, or the morpho butterflies of the New World. The butterfly has a coiled double tube, or proboscis, that functions like a double-barrelled drinking straw, which it uses to suck up nectar from flowers.

Nectar nightshift

While a few day-flying moths, such as the zodiac and four o'clock moths of Australia, visit flowers during the day, most moths are active at night. There are many of them: Australia is graced with about 390 species of butterfly, but has nearly 22 000 known species of moth, including the giant Hercules moth and the many hawkmoth species. Rain-forest hawkmoths, like hummingbirds, hover in front of flowers, probing for nectar with their long proboscis. The moth with the longest proboscis – extending to 30–35 cm in length – is Morgan's sphinx moth of Madagascar's

FLYING JEWEL *A crowned woodnymph hummingbird drinks nectar from a Heliconia flower and has its head dusted with pollen.*

KINGDOMS OF MONKEYS

BORNEO

ACCORDING TO ONE THEORY, ABOUT 55 MILLION YEARS AGO, DURING A PERIOD OF RAPID GLOBAL WARMING, A NEW GROUP OF ANIMALS APPEARED IN SOUTHERN ASIA. In just 25 000 years they had spread throughout the world.
They were the earliest primates, ancestors of monkeys, apes and humans. They had forward-facing eyes for three-dimensional vision, large brains, hands specialised for gripping and manipulating food and nails instead of claws. Some types of primate developed colour vision, a trait that may have co-evolved with the production of colourful fruits by rain-forest trees. Two groups came to dominate the rain forests – Old World monkeys in Africa and Asia and New World monkeys in South America.

About 2 million years ago, the climate of the Congo and neighbouring regions changed. It became drier, and monkeys living in the rain forests there had three choices – migrate, adapt or wait it out. The macaques moved away and spread across Asia. The baboons adapted to the drier conditions, moving down to the ground and out across the savannah. The guenons remained in the fragmented gallery forests beside rivers and waited. When the climate improved again and the trees returned, they went on to fill every ecological niche in the Congo rain forest.

In southern Asia today, the rain forests are home to several species of macaques, each occupying its own level in the forest. In south-west India, the extremely rare lion-

MONKEY FOREST Borneo is the domain of the macaques. Each species occupies a different level in the rain forest, where fruits and seeds make up about 90 per cent of their diet, but they will try almost anything that is remotely edible.

The talapoins of Gabon have been seen diving for fish. Youngsters learn what is edible and what is not by watching their mothers.

tailed macaque feeds on fruit in the trees, while the Bonnet macaque forages mostly on the ground. In Sumatra and Borneo, the robust southern pig-tailed macaque occupies the lower levels, while the relatively small long-tailed macaque plucks buds and young leaves from the highest branches in the canopy. The long-tailed macaque is also at home fishing for crustaceans in rivers, earning itself the alternative name 'crab-eating macaque'. Both species live in complex groups in which they communicate with a body language that includes yawning, lip smacking and eyebrow flashing.

Two other groups in the rain forests of South-east Asia are the langurs and the leaf monkeys. The delicate silvered leaf monkey and spectacled leaf monkey feed on the leaves and seeds of legumes. They have an unusual stomach partitioned into sacs that enable them to digest their fibre-rich, toxin-high diet. Adult silver-leaf monkeys have a shaggy black-and-silver coat, but their offspring are bright orange for the first three months.

African omnivores

The primary food of the guenon monkeys is fruit, but they will eat just about anything that is edible – seeds, flowers, buds, leaves, bark, gum, resins, roots, bulbs, tubers, rhizomes, insects, spiders, slugs and snails, freshwater crabs, frogs, lizards, small birds, rats and mice. One group – the talapoins of Gabon – have even been seen diving for fish. Youngsters learn what is edible and what is not by watching their mothers.

Nutritionally poor forest sites accommodate just one guenon species, while richer places might have two or more species living in harmony. Blue monkeys and Sykes monkeys, for example, are of a similar size and build and eat the same foods, so they generally do not live together. Blue monkeys and red-tailed monkeys differ in the way they feed and the food they eat, so they are often found side by side. The larger blue monkeys tend to hang out under a closed forest canopy, where they eat leaves, while the less robust red-tails like tangles of branches in which they can hide from monkey-eating eagles. They are frequently joined by the even smaller mona monkeys, which eat more insects, such as grasshoppers, than the other two species. The greater the number of alert eyes in a group, the more likely a predator will be spotted before it becomes a danger.

Each guenon species has evolved distinct face colours, expressions and body signals to communicate with others of its own kind. In some regions, monkeys of different species communicate, and even cooperate.

PLANT SNACK A mother pig-tailed macaque and her infant, in Borneo. These macaques feed on 160 different kinds of plants.

In south-western Côte d'Ivoire, seven species have been seen together – three guenons, olive colobus monkeys, red colobus and sooty mangabeys. They get together for protection: one of the guenons – the Diana monkey – is an especially good lookout.

Diana monkeys are known for their alertness, and olive colobus monkeys stay near them almost permanently. The Diana monkeys feed at all forest levels, but the olive colobus stay in the lower levels, minimising competition. From time to time, red colobus monkeys join them, usually for protection when chimpanzees are hunting in packs. When hunting is out of season, such as between September and November, the red colobus go their own way.

Miniature monkeys

South and Central America's largest monkeys are the howlers, which are almost exclusively leaf-eaters, and the woolly monkeys, which have a mixed diet of fruit and leaves. The New World forests are also home to a collection of much smaller monkeys – the marmosets and tamarins. These species feed on whatever is abundant. Tree flowers are a favourite. Emperor tamarins eat nectar without damaging the flowers, and because their faces become covered in pollen they are unwitting pollinators. But mixed troops of moustached tamarins and saddle-backed tamarins destroy flowers. Once a troop was seen to consume 44 000 flowers from ten *Symphonia* trees in six weeks.

The smallest of the New World monkeys is the pygmy marmoset, with a head and body just 18 cm long. It is the world's smallest monkey and it has the most unusual diet – it uses its sharp teeth to make incisions in the bark of trees and then licks the gum that oozes out of the wound. In the understorey, saddle-backed tamarins and moustached tamarins catch insects coming to drink the nectar from flowers, and the agile, squirrel-like Goelding's monkey eats fruits, insects or even small mammals. When food is plentiful it forages in a small area, but when times are hard it expands its range. It can jump big gaps between trees, staying upright and twisting in mid-air to land feet first. One of the greatest leapers is the white-faced saki, also known as 'flying Jack'. It speeds through the lower parts of the canopy and understorey, leaping horizontally between trees. The female is a dull brown that blends in with the forest, but the male has a stark white face. Its conspicuous colour is thought to draw predators away from females and young.

The saki monkeys are seed-predators, so the rain-forest trees cannot rely on them for seed dispersal. They have sharp canines for breaking into fruit and nuts and tough cheek teeth to

ROYAL CONNECTIONS The emperor tamarin's diet includes nectar, fruit and other plant matter, insects and frogs.

AFRICA

ALERT FEEDER A Diana monkey keeps an eye out for predators. It can store foraged food in cheek pouches to eat later. Like most guenon species, it is threatened by the loss of Africa's rain forests.

crush them, destroying the seeds. They also seek out younger seeds, which are richer in nutrients. When the seeds are forming, saki monkeys wake early and move from their sleeping trees to one of 50 or more favourite feeding trees, such as the breadnut tree. Black-handed spider monkeys and Geoffroy's tamarins, on the other hand, help trees disperse their seeds – when they eat fruit, the seeds pass through their guts unharmed.

Many New World monkeys are not exclusively vegetarian, but take insects and spiders when they are plentiful. White-faced sakis are partial to wasps. Normally they utter food calls to tell the rest of the troop where the best pickings are, but when they find a wasps' nest they keep quiet and eat as many wasps as they can before the others find out.

FRUIT AND NUT CASES

FIG-EATERS Sulawesi red-knobbed hornbills live on figs and a variety of other fruit, which they gather from the top of the canopy. They are important seed dispersers.

IF A TREE'S SEEDS DROP DIRECTLY ONTO THE GROUND BELOW, THE OFFSPRING WILL BE IN DIRECT COMPETITION WITH THE PARENT. To ensure that their seeds are more widely dispersed, some trees produce fruit or nuts with which to bribe animals into providing a distribution service. Over 70 per cent of rain-forest plants have fleshy fruit that are attractive to animals, so their seeds are not only carried away safe inside the fruit-eater's gut, but are deposited some distance away, with a dollop of fertiliser to help germination. The droppings create a microsite of moisture and extra nutrients, a useful asset in the competitive rain-forest environment.

Trees use colour and smell to attract animals. Bright red, black, yellow or blue fruit tends to attract animals that rely mainly on vision to find food, such as birds and monkeys. These may not be the actual colours of the fruit as seen by the foragers, because some animals, such as birds and insects, see a wider spectrum of colours than we do.

Small fruits are attractive to a wide range of species and a great number of individuals. They tend to have a single, large seed that can be swallowed in one gulp. Most birds that eat berries and small fruit swallow them whole, so the seeds are not damaged on their passage through the gut, although some rain-forest pigeons have tough gizzards and the seeds that they eat are destroyed. Parrots tend to break up seeds before swallowing them, even the toughest ones. In the Queensland rain forest, the seeds of the maple *Flindersia* can be found in pieces on the ground despite the protection of a hard shell and sharp tubercles, as cockatoos destroy them.

Larger fruits have fewer dispersers. They tend to contain many small seeds, which are dispersed by animals that have teeth and chew food, such as mammals. By producing many seeds, the plant ensures that at least a few pass through unscathed.

Forest elephants in the Congo break into hard-shelled fruits, such as those of the Makore tree or African cherry. The plant is so dependent on them for dispersal, it is only found in forests where elephants are living. The young plants sprout from elephant dung piles, along with 50 or so other rain-forest plants. The elephants ensure they are in the right place at the right time to take advantage of the various trees in fruit by having a network of trails through the forest. The trail intersections occur where the elephants' favourite trees grow. Elephants in these forests are vital seed dispersers – in fact they are responsible for dispersing the seeds of nearly half of all the tall rain-forest trees in West and Central Africa, the remainder being spread by hornbills and monkeys. If the elephants were eliminated, many rain-forest plants would disappear with them.

Smaller forest residents are less obvious dispersers. Scatter-hoarders, such as the white-tailed rat and musky rat kangaroo of Australian rain forests, bury seeds for later use; if they forget where they have left a store, the seeds germinate.

Fruit-eating birds

Many rain-forest birds rely on fruit and little else for food. They tend to select fruits that are rich in fats and proteins, such as plants of the laurel family, the most familiar being avocado. These fruit specialists have wide, soft-walled gizzards, so seeds pass through the gut less altered and more viable. Also, any protective poisons in the seed coat are less likely to be released. The less specialised birds feed on less nutritious fruits that are high in sugar and water content, obtaining their fats and proteins from other sources, such as insects.

Generally, seeds take between ten minutes and two hours to pass through a bird's digestive system. As birds are active and mobile and do not remain for long in one tree, the chances are that they will have moved away from the parent tree before voiding the seeds. This makes birds ideal seed dispersers. But plants do not take chances. Some add a laxative to their fruit so seeds are ejected before digestive juices have had time to act on them.

WIDE-RANGING PIGEON The thick-billed green pigeon is a species of Indo-Pacific ground dove found throughout southern Asia, from India to the Philippines. It inhabits tropical lowland forests and mangrove forests, and feeds on fruit.

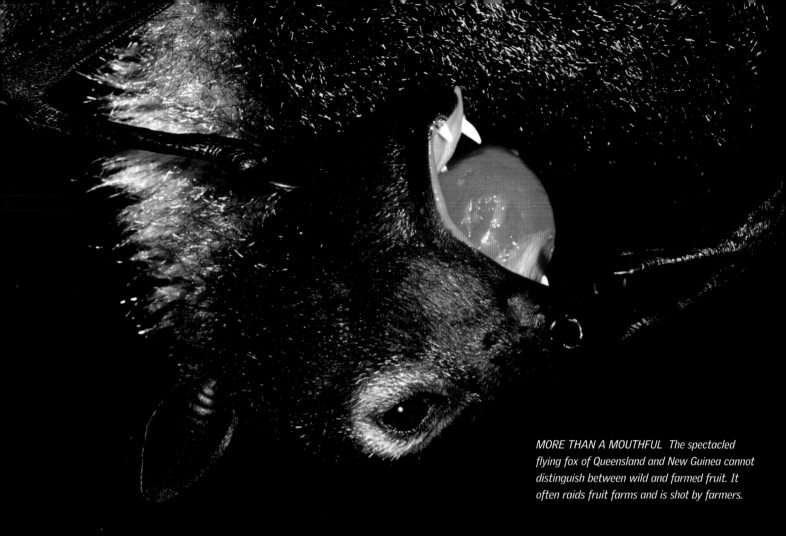

MORE THAN A MOUTHFUL The spectacled flying fox of Queensland and New Guinea cannot distinguish between wild and farmed fruit. It often raids fruit farms and is shot by farmers.

In the Congo, hornbills disperse about 22 per cent of seeds of rain-forest trees, making them the second most important rain-forest seed dispersers after forest elephants. In Cameroon, for example, just two species of hornbill – the black-casqued and white-thighed hornbills – are responsible for carrying the seeds of a quarter of the 300 known species of rain-forest trees. The hornbill's gut is kind to seeds and almost any that pass through are capable of germination. Seeds remain in the gut for 50 minutes or more, and are deposited at least 500 m from the parent tree. The plant makes its seeds attractive by producing a fleshy outer coat that is lightweight yet rich in high-energy oils.

Hornbills have an unusual nesting behaviour. The male bird incarcerates the female and her offspring in a tree hollow by partially blocking the entrance with mud. Sealed in her cell, the female is totally dependent on the male for food. He brings rain-forest fruit to the nest and regurgitates them for his mate. The family is safe in their nest from tree snakes and other predators, but if the male is captured or killed, his partner and offspring inevitably die, unable to escape from a nest that becomes a prison.

In New Guinean and Australian rain forests, pigeons such as the Torres imperial pigeon are important seed dispersers. They eat fruit and berries almost exclusively, retaining seeds inside the gut for up to four hours. They might fly 30 km or more between roosting and feeding sites, so seeds are carried far from the parent tree. Bowerbirds and birds of paradise are also effective seed dispersers, but the single most important bird is the southern cassowary, which feeds on fruits that have dropped to the ground. In Queensland, the fruits of 200 or more rain-forest plants are known to be eaten by cassowaries. In one study the seeds from 78 species were found in cassowary droppings, 70 of which passed through the gut unharmed and remained viable. Cassowaries have large territories, often several kilometres across, and seeds take up to ten hours to pass through their gut, so a bird might have travelled a considerable distance in a day, dispersing seeds far and wide.

Nocturnal fruit cases

Mammals that feed when light levels are low, such as at dawn or dusk and at night, tend to feed on less brightly coloured but more juicy fruits. They rely on smell more than vision to find their food. This is true of the fruit bats, or flying foxes. While birds tend to select oily fruits, the bats prefer sugary ones, so it is no surprise that they eat the same fruit as people and are therefore labelled as pests. Nevertheless, they are important seed dispersers. The spectacled flying fox, which lives in Queensland's rain forests, travels over 40 km each night between roosting and feeding sites, and carries the seeds of over 23 rain-forest plants. It plays the same role as monkeys in a forest where there are no monkeys, relying on site and smell to locate the best fruits. Fruit bats are reliant on fruit all year round, so they are confined to the tropics.

Fruits bats roost in huge numbers, their hanging, pod-like outlines decorating favourite rain-forest trees. The bats fight for the best sites, the more dominant individuals occupying the highest and safest branches and the weaker bats roosting on the lower, more exposed ones. Sentries are posted to warn the colony of danger, and if the roost is put to flight, clouds of flapping bats can darken the sky.

Fruit bats are found in the rain forests of Madagascar, the Indian sub-continent, South-east Asia, New Guinea and Australasia, but they are absent from the New World. In the Americas, the large spear-nosed bats, some species with a 60 cm wingspan, have adopted the fruit bat's way of life. They also drink nectar, catch insects and will even intercept smaller, insect-eating bats and eat them.

Surprising fruit-eaters

Birds and bats are well-known fruit-eaters, but reptiles are not renowned for fruit-eating habits. Two exceptions are Boyd's forest dragon in Queensland and freshwater turtles in South America, which occasionally eat fleshy fruits and disperse seeds.

With so much water in rain forests, including many streams and rivers, several trees rely on water to help with seed dispersal. In Queensland, for example, the seedpods of the black bean and the buoyant, red-coloured berries of the scrub cherry, or lilly pilly, float well. Both are brightly coloured to attract animals, but are often seen floating along in streams. The bright red fruit of the black

palm is sometimes carried overland by flowing water. In some places fish eat fruit and help disperse the seeds. In Queensland, for example, the jungle perch has been seen to eat figs.

Rotting fruit

While many rain-forest creatures prefer young or ripe fruit, there are a few that wait for it to rot and even ferment. Fallen fruit contains high concentrations of sugars and nitrogen, dietary components sought by some forest butterflies, including the blue morpho, cracker and owl butterflies of South America and the evening brown butterfly of Australia and New Guinea. Instead of seeking nectar from flowers, they locate fallen fruit, and it seems to give them an advantage: fruit-feeding butterflies live longer than nectar-feeding ones. In tropical forest in Uganda, for example, *Euphaedra* butterflies – large butterflies that flop around in the understorey – have been known to live for 293 days, whereas most adult butterflies live for a few days at most.

At night, some species of moth, such as the fruit-sucking noctuid moth *Othreis* of Australia and New Guinea, are attracted to ripe and overripe fruits. It is a large moth, with a 10 cm

FRUIT JUICE Rotting fruit is a magnet for forest butterflies. They sip the juices using their long proboscis.

wingspan, but its most important feature is its proboscis. It has a 2.5 cm long, modified proboscis that can pierce the skins of fruit, enabling it to suck out the juices from the inside. The moth also carries a fungus that rots fruit. The wound produced by the moth is subsequently infected with the fungus, which releases a penetrating odour attractive to other moths. Noctuid moths without the modified proboscis can then feed from the juices that ooze from the wound.

Fig specialists

Figs are produced all year round, so they are key species for rain-forest animals. Many animals feed on them, but some have become fig specialists, such as the aptly named fig parrot and fig bird from Queensland, the latter with eyes so sensitive to the colour of figs that it can tell whether fruit is unripe, ripe or over-ripe and subtle changes in between. Different figs target different types of animal. Figs that attract bats tend to be green when ripe and are packed with carbohydrates and protein, whereas those that are interesting to birds are generally red and less rich in nutrients. The frequency of fruiting and the place on the tree where fruit are found also varies. Bat figs tend to be produced in one mammoth fruiting episode, whereas bird figs fruit over a long period; and figs produced on the trunk, rather than the branches, are easier for bats to access.

Greater and lesser apes

In South-east Asia, the coming of the rains marks the fruiting season of many rain-forest trees, including the sweet-tasting salak and the sour rambutan, but one of the most sought-after fruits is the durian. Orang-utans on the islands of Borneo and Sumatra love durians, despite the fruit's extraordinary smell that people find revolting. The orang-utans are so addicted they will wait beside a tree each night for the fruit to ripen and fall. About 60 per cent of an orang-utan's diet is fruit, including mangoes, figs and lychees as well as durian. They also consume shoots, leaves, tree bark, insects and mineral-rich soil.

The name *orang-utan* means 'man of the forest', and these apes are recognised instantly by their long, red fur and long arms. Their arms can span up to 2 m from fingertip to fingertip. They are strong arms, too, whereas their legs are relatively short and weak. Most of the orang-utan's strength is in its arms and shoulders, and it gets about by swinging through the forest. This behaviour, known as brachiating, is shown to perfection by the orang-utan's distant relatives, the gibbons.

Gibbons are known as lesser apes. They are less robust than orang-utans, and are probably the most agile non-flying creatures in the forest. The gibbon's wrist has a ball-and-socket joint and the arms are long, enabling these creatures to move with remarkable speed through the treetops, crossing gaps up to 10 m wide. Fruit makes up half their diet, but they will munch on leaves and flowers and catch the occasional insect.

FOREST ELEPHANT

SMALLER THAN ITS EAST AFRICAN COUSIN,

THE FOREST ELEPHANT MORE THAN MAKES UP IN ATTITUDE WHAT IT LACKS IN SIZE. It is exceptionally aggressive and will not hesitate to chase any humans it sees as a threat and skewer them into the ground. Males tend to be solitary; females forage in relatively small groups, sometimes consisting of just a mother and her offspring. Larger groups get together in forest clearings, known as bais, where they dig into the ground with their tusks and pick up soil with their trunks. The soil contains essential minerals that are absent from the rest of the elephants' diet.

One of their favourite foods is the *Omphalocarpum* fruit. It is about the size of a melon, round and brown, and it grows on the trunk of the tree rather than in the branches. The elephants' acute hearing, together with sensitivity to low-frequency sounds, can detect the thump made by falling fruit hitting the ground, and animals come running from all parts of the forest. They sometimes stab the fruit with their tusks to get at the edible material inside. At the centre is a sticky sap, a bit like chewing gum, and flat seeds that pass unharmed through the elephants' gut. The relationship between the tree and the elephant is so close that wherever poachers kill elephants, the fruits rot on the ground and seeds fail to germinate.

VITAL STATISTICS

ORDER: Proboscidea
SPECIES: *Loxodona cyclotis*
HABITAT: Dense lowland rain forest
DISTRIBUTION: Central and West Africa
KEY FEATURES: Down-turning tusks; ears more rounded than savannah elephants; the elephants' smaller size suits it for forest life.

RAIN-FOREST DWARFS

HIDDEN IN THE DEPTHS OF THE RAIN FORESTS ARE MINIATURE VERSIONS OF SOME OF THE WORLD'S LARGEST HERBIVORES. Their small size is an adaptation to the requirements of living in a restricted forest environment. Shy, nocturnal and rarely seen, these species spend much of their time in the relative safety of dense undergrowth. As they feed after dark, they depend on a highly developed sense of smell, rather than sight, for finding food.

Scaled-down giants

There is a small subspecies of the African forest elephant – the pygmy elephant of Cameroon; and on the island of Borneo there is a dwarf version of the Asian elephant – the Borneo pygmy elephant. Borneo's miniature pachyderm is confined to the north-east of the island and not many more than 1000 are thought to be alive in the wild today.

In the rain forests of Java, Sumatra and Borneo the local rhinoceros species are significantly smaller than their African or Indian cousins. The Sumatran rhino is the smallest and one of the most endangered rhino species. It is closely related to the extinct woolly rhino, and has coarse red hair. Unlike other Asian rhinos, the Sumatran rhino has two horns, the front one longer than the rear. Its skin is folded into armour-like plates. It generally lives alone in dense rain forest and is active mainly at night. It has hooked, prehensile lips, which it uses to clasp fruit and vegetation, consuming about 50 kg of food a day. Borneo has a miniature version of the Sumatran rhino, the smallest known rhino subspecies. There are fewer than 100 Sumatran rhinos surviving in the wild. It has long been hunted for its horn, which is used in Chinese traditional medicine and thought to be more potent than African rhino horn.

The Javan rhino is hairless with a single horn and grey skin hanging in folds, like the Sumatran rhino. It survives in only two places – on the Indonesian island of Java and in Vietnam. It is a solitary browser and grazer, and prefers lowland forest areas with a good supply of water and mud wallows, where it covers itself in mud to protect against biting insects. Human activity has pushed it into highland areas where thick bamboo and rattan dominate. It is the most endangered rhino species, with fewer than 10 known individuals in Vietnam and about 60 in Java.

Asian teddy

The rain forests of South-east Asia are also home to the world's smallest bear – the Asian sun bear. Standing on its hind legs it is barely 1.2 m tall. Short, sleek brown or black hair covers most of its body – an adaptation to its lowland rain-forest habitat – with a pale orange horseshoe-shaped mark on its chest. Its muzzle is also pale orange-yellow. The sun bear is mainly nocturnal, resting in a tree by day. It has large paws with naked soles and lightweight, sickle-shaped claws, which enable it to climb well, but give it an awkward pigeon-toed gait on the ground. It has poor eyesight, and uses its keen sense of smell to find food.

Like all bears, the sun bear is an omnivore. Its mixed diet consists of lizards, birds and small mammals, birds' eggs, earthworms, termites, fruits, berries, shoots, roots and coconuts. It has strong jaws, which it uses to crack open tough nuts, and a very long

LOW-LEVEL FEEDER The rare Javan rhino is a browser. It uses its prehensile lips to grab hold of food and sometimes knocks down saplings in order to reach leaves on the higher branches.

SMALL BEAR Sun bears, the world's smallest bears, live in the lowland tropical rain forests of South-east Asia. They are good tree-climbers, and sleep in the branches by day.

RELATIVE SIZES Some tropical rain-forest mammals are smaller and less robust than their equivalents in open habitats, an adaptation to moving about in the more restricted environment of the forest floor.

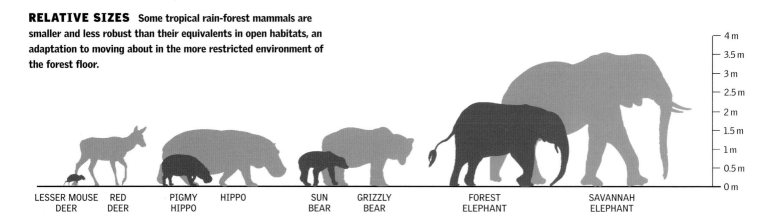

| LESSER MOUSE DEER | RED DEER | PIGMY HIPPO | HIPPO | SUN BEAR | GRIZZLY BEAR | FOREST ELEPHANT | SAVANNAH ELEPHANT |

tongue, which enables it to reach honey and insects inside tree cavities. Its taste for honey gave rise to the sun bear's local Malay and Indonesian name *beruang madu*, meaning honey bear.

Sun bears, like many rain-forest animals, are threatened by habitat loss and poaching, both for meat and for medicines. In Chinese traditional medicine various parts of the bear's anatomy are believed to have healing properties, although herbal alternatives exist that are cheaper to obtain and just as beneficial.

Diminutive deer and antelope

Relatively unchanged for 5 million years, the tiny mouse deer, or chevrotain, lives a solitary existence in African, Indian and South-east Asian rain forests. The largest of the four living species, Africa's water chevrotain is 85 cm long and stands just 35 cm at the shoulder; the smallest, Asia's lesser mouse deer, is only 45 cm long. None have horns or antlers, but both sexes have enlarged upper canines, the male's sabre-like teeth projecting down on either side of its lower jaw. They have powerful hindquarters and slender legs, and walk with the head down so they can tunnel through thick vegetation. Chevrotains are active mainly at night. Nearly three-quarters of their diet consists of fallen fruits, but they also eat leaves and occasionally take insects, crayfish and even small mammals.

Africa's rain forests also harbour small to medium-sized antelopes known as duikers, from the Afrikaans word for 'diver', a reference to the way they dive into vegetation at the slightest hint of danger. They are mainly browsers, feeding on fruits, nuts, leaves, shoots, seeds, buds, flowers

ELUSIVE HIPPOS The shy, nocturnal pygmy hippopotamus is rarely seen and little studied in the wild. Europeans were unaware of its existence until the 1870s.

*MINIATURE DEER The lesser mouse deer is a
small, secretive inhabitant of the tropical rain
forests of Africa and Asia. Weighing about 2 kg,
it is the world's smallest known hoofed animal.*

and bark. Like chevrotains, they sometimes eat meat, munching
on snails and catching insects and small mammals. They also feed
on carrion. There are 24 recognised species, 13 of them forest
duikers that have shorter legs than their bush-living cousins.
They stand about 36–46 cm at the shoulder, and the males have
small, spiky horns.

Pygmy hippos

The rain forests of West Africa are home to the extremely rare
pygmy hippopotamus. For a hippo it is very small, standing no more
than 0.8 m at the shoulder and measuring about 1.5 m long – about
half the size of its East African cousin. It has a smaller head and
longer legs in proportion to its body than its larger relative. Little
is known about the pygmy hippo's habits and behaviour, but it is
thought to be solitary, rarely meeting others of its own kind. It lives
in areas of dense vegetation close to swamps and streams, and
moves along well-worn trails used by several hippos, but by a
system of dung-marking avoids meeting its own species except at
mating time. The pygmy hippo is a herbivore and feeds in and out

of water, digging up roots and swamp plants and taking leaves
from trees and shrubs. It also eats shoots and fruits, which it
crushes with very strong teeth.

Miniature cattle

The mountain and lowland anoas are two species of small wild
cattle that live on the Indonesian island of Sulawesi and the
neighbouring island of Butung. They resemble tiny water buffalo,
and their name, anoa, is the Celebes (Sulawesi) word for buffalo.
They stand no more than 75 cm high at the shoulder, making
them no larger than sheep. Indeed, the lowland anoa is one of
the world's smallest species of cattle. Both species inhabit
undisturbed forest, the lowland anoa in swamp forests and the
mountain anoa in montane rain forests.

   Anoas are active in the early morning, feeding on grass,
fruits, leaves, herbs, saplings and low-growing plants, and rest in
the shade during the heat of the day. They wallow in mud to help
them keep cool. There are reports of them drinking seawater to
obtain additional minerals.

   Like the other miniature mammals, anoas have been
hunted to the edge of extinction. No more than 3000 of each
species are thought to be living in the rain-forests today. It has
been considered endangered since 1960, and those few that have
survived are threatened by continued habitat loss.

WITH SO MUCH PLANT FOOD DROPPING FROM THE CANOPY, THE FOREST FLOOR IS A RICH FORAGING GROUND FOR HERBIVORES. A number of plant-eating animals have become giants, rather than dwarfs, on the abundant pickings of leaves, fruits, berries and nuts. And just as large herbivores, such as cattle, have dwarf representatives in the rain forest, so some anatomically smaller families, such as rodents, have come to be represented

LARGE HERBIVORES

here by giants. The South American capybara is the world's largest known rodent. Up to 1.4 m long and 62 cm at the shoulder – roughly the size of a labrador – it is widespread throughout the continent, including the Amazon and other New World rain forests. Capybaras generally live in large groups. Their feet are partially webbed, reflecting the fact that they spend much of their time in or near water. They graze on grasses and aquatic plants, feeding mainly in the morning. They then spend the rest of the day digesting, often wallowing in water to escape the tropical heat during the warmest parts of the day.

Africa's forests boast the world's largest wild pig – the giant forest hog, up to 2 m long and 1 m at the shoulder. During the heat of midday, a group – or 'sounder' – of up to 20 hogs occupies elaborate nests of woven vegetation. At dawn and dusk, they travel well-worn tracks to clearings and neighbouring savannah to feed. Large males defend the group against leopards and hyenas, and will attack people, too.

West and Central African rain forests also ring to the squeals of a slightly smaller pig species, the red river hog or bush pig. It is recognised by its foxy red coat, black-and-white markings on the head and tassels on its ears. In January and February, groups of sometimes 100 or more hogs – along with many other large forest herbivores – seek out the avocado-sized fruits of the moabi tree. These drop with an audible thump, and when they break open they release a strong yeasty smell that attracts hogs from all around.

DISTINCTIVE SNOUT The Brazilian tapir (left) grazes food on the riverbed. By day it keeps cool by bathing and also uses rivers and lakes to find refuge from predators, such as jaguars.

FOREST CAMOUFLAGE The okapi's stripes help young okapis to follow their mothers in the dark forest. They also act as camouflage, breaking up the animal's outline.

Left in the forest

Several large mammals in West and Central Africa found themselves in the rain forests because of climate change – natural climate change that took place over thousands of years and gradually caught them in the 'wrong' place. They include antelope, such as the bongo and sitatunga – long-legged, fast-running creatures that would seem more at home on the savannah. Over the eons, they were trapped by the expanding forests and so settled down to a life in the slow lane. Similarly, the okapi, a relative of the giraffe, became a forest-dweller. It has a brown velvet coat and striped legs, like pyjamas, that help it blend in with the foliage. It is so good at hiding that its very existence was unknown to biologists until 1901.

In South-east Asia, the forests of Cambodia, Laos and Vietnam have also kept their secrets. Recent discoveries have included several species of wild cattle and deer, such as the kouprey, recognised in 1937, and the saola or Vu Quang ox, discovered as recently as 1992. The saola was first identified from sets of spindle-shaped horns collected at markets on the Vietnam–Laos border. Only 11 individuals have ever been seen.

There are four species of tapir living today – three in Latin America and one in Malaysia. Despite a pig-like size and appearance, tapirs are related to horses and rhinos. Their main feature is a short, highly mobile nose that can grab foliage, but they also eat a range of other rain-forest foods, including fallen fruit. They tend to be solitary, are usually found close to water and can swim well.

GIANT GUINEA PIGS Capybaras have eyes and noses on the tops of their heads. This allows them to remain submerged, yet still be alert for predators and continue to breathe.

LEAF-EATERS

WHILE MANY RAIN-FOREST HERBIVORES ARE OCCASIONAL LEAF-EATERS, A FEW ARE LEAF SPECIALISTS. They thrive on the diet, but it presents certain difficulties. One is that leaves are not very rich in nutrients, so these animals have to eat vast quantities of them to obtain what they need. Another is that leaves tend to be laced with poisonous chemicals – an attempt by the plant to prevent animals eating them. As a result, creatures eating large quantities of leaves are potentially exposing themselves to large amounts of poisons.

At first, a tree focuses more on growth and less on defence, so young leaves tend to have fewer poisons; as a leaf matures it becomes more noxious. The rubber tree, for example, produces sap like latex that gums up insect mouthparts. Other trees produce substances that block protein absorption or interfere with the nervous system. The specialist leaf-eaters have found ways to circumnavigate plant defences and neutralise the poisons.

One such creature is a very unusual bird – the hoatzin, which lives in the Amazon's flooded forest (see pages 140–144). The hoatzin is extraordinary even to look at. It has an electric-blue face and punk-like plumage on its head. It also swims before it can fly, and when it does fly it resembles a bloated chicken. Yet it survives in the forest. Among its special adaptations are a huge crop – a pouch near the throat that serves as a temporary storage place for undigested leaves. When this is full, the bird has to rest its breast against a branch to stay upright. Unique among birds, the hoatzin has a foregut similar to that of cattle and sheep. Bacteria in its foregut break down the leaves it has eaten, releasing the nutrients inside.

Because the leaves are packed with strongly aromatic chemicals, the hoatzin also smells strongly, giving rise to its local name, 'stinkbird'. The stink sometimes attracts nest predators, such as capuchin monkeys, but hoatzin chicks have a novel way to escape. Their nests are usually on boughs that overhang the river, so the chicks simply drop into the water, wait for the danger to pass and then clamber back to the nest using special claws on their wings.

Poisonous leaves

Among the poisons that trees use to protect their leaves are tannins, strychnine and cyanide, but several canopy animals have digestive systems that neutralise these. Special bacteria in the guts of African colobus monkeys, for example, enable them to eat as much cyanide in a single day as would kill a human.

Another monkey with a unique digestive system is the proboscis monkey, which lives in swampy rain forests in coastal areas of Borneo and the Mentawai Islands off Sumatra's western

ONE OF A KIND The hoatzin or 'stinkbird' is such a strange creature it has been classified in a family of its own. Scientists are not at all sure which birds are its nearest living relatives.

NOSEY MONKEY Although large for a monkey, the nose of the female proboscis monkey is still much smaller than the male's. Proboscis monkeys are accomplished swimmers – they have been found swimming a mile out at sea.

coast. Its stomach is divided into compartments, each with cellulose-digesting bacteria that help to digest leaves and neutralise toxins. Because the monkeys need to consume such huge quantities of the leaves, they look permanently pregnant – their stomach contents account for a quarter of their body weight.

Proboscis monkeys get their name from the large, pendulous nose sported by the males. The reason for the large nose is unclear, but it becomes red and engorged when the animal is excited or angry. It also acts as a resonator when the monkey makes its honking call, warning of danger.

The monkeys generally live in groups of 10 to 30 individuals dominated by a large male. These troops crash through the trees, with monkeys catapulting themselves up to 40 m between tree crowns. When they reach water and the gap is too wide to clear in a single jump, they simply belly flop into the water and then either doggy paddle or wade upright to the far bank.

Howlers and bounders

In South and Central American rain forests, the howler monkeys occupy a similar niche to the proboscis monkey. Green leaves, both tender young ones and tougher older leaves that contain more nutrients, provide about 40 per cent of their diet – the rest consists of fruits, buds, flowers and nuts. Cellulose-digesting bacteria in their guts break the leaves down. The monkeys feast in the morning and then spend the rest of the day lying about while their digestive system deals with the meal. On occasions, leaves are the only food available. In these lean times, howlers select the most nutrient-rich leaves and move slowly to conserve energy.

The ringtail possum and Lumholtz tree-kangaroo or boongary are leaf-eaters of the Australian rain forests. Tree kangaroos evolved from terrestrial kangaroos and wallabies, developing longer tails for balance and stronger forelimbs for climbing. As with the hoatzin, leaves are broken down in a forestomach – a series of bacteria-containing tubular sacs that precedes the true stomach. Tree kangaroos chew the cud, but unlike cattle and sheep, they do not produce methane. Instead, they produce acetate that further helps the digestion of leaves.

LEAFY DIET Colobus monkeys have a multi-chambered stomach where bacteria break down the cellulose in plant cell walls, releasing the nutrients inside them.

DIETARY SUPPLEMENTS

MANY ANIMALS LIVING IN THE RAIN FOREST WOULD EXPERIENCE DIETARY DEFICIENCIES if they stuck rigidly to their normal diet of leaves, fruits or seeds. In order to supplement their diets, they eat earthy substances such as clay – a practice known as geophagy. Like gorillas and chimpanzees, Africa's forest elephants will eat soil, resulting in large treeless clearings where they have turned the ground over with their tusks. These mineral 'licks', as they are known, are found where igneous rocks intrude between the sedimentary layers. The clay soils here contain significantly higher quantities of sodium, potassium, calcium, magnesium, phosphorus and manganese compared with other soils. The clay itself might also help to absorb or neutralise plant poisons.

The benefits of clay

In South and Central America, parrots and macaws tend to eat fruits when they are still unripe. This is one way to beat the rush when the tree's fruits eventually ripen, but unripe fruits contain more poisons than ripe ones. To neutralise these poisons, parrots and macaws congregate at licks in riverbanks and eat clay. These 'meetings' in the Amazon rain forest follow a strict routine. At dawn the smaller birds, such as blue-headed parrots and mealy parrots, usually arrive first, followed by the larger macaws. The birds socialise at first, but if no more than 20 birds turn up they abandon the visit and disperse. If they have a quorum, sometimes a minimum of 300 birds, they begin to circle several times and then, one by one, drop down to the clay lick. With the brave pioneers on the lick face, the rest of the congregation piles in.

Upwards of 300 brightly coloured macaws and over a thousand Amazon parrots, all chattering noisily, might be feeding at the lick at any one time. They are constantly wary of predators and will take flight at the slightest hint of danger. A small landslide might cause one of the birds to scream and they will all take to the air at once. Returning to the lick they use their strong bills to break off and then eat small, knuckle-sized chunks of clay.

The birds risk being on the ground in this way in order to eat clay that is rich in the mineral kaolin – the same ingredient used in some stomach medicines. The small, negatively charged clay particles bind to the positively charged plant poisons, which stops them being absorbed, so they pass harmlessly through the bird's gut. In this way, the plant poisons are effectively neutralised. The clays are also rich in sodium, providing the birds with a supplementary mineral 'pill' whenever they visit the lick. Clay or salt licks are magnets for birds in rain forests in other parts of the world, too. The African grey parrot frequents licks in West and Central Africa, and in Papua New Guinea cockatoos, hornbills, pigeons and cassowaries are all known visitors.

CLAY MEAL A green-winged or red-and-green macaw nibbles on a chunk of clay extracted from a riverbank at Manu in the Peruvian Amazon.

Hanging out at the lick

In the forests of Central and South America, acrobatic spider monkeys gather in the trees around a lick and, as their confidence grows, they gradually come down to the ground. At first they hang by their powerful prehensile tails over the lick and grab handfuls of mud. Usually they eat as much as they can in the shortest possible time, but sometimes they throw caution to the wind and romp about in the semi-liquid mud like mud wrestlers, getting covered from head to toe in mud. When the monkeys

DOWN TO EARTH African forest elephants visit clearings or 'bais' where they dig down with their tusks and take up mineral-rich soil to supplement their diet.

have gone, tapirs, peccaries, deer and various rain-forest birds and bats take their place. The monkeys and the tapirs mine the clay in the same place, following mineral-rich seams in the soil, like miners tunnelling in a coalmine.

Forest predators such as pumas and jaguars stake out muddy clay licks, and are a constant threat. Other dangers come in the shape of boa constrictors in the trees and spectacled caiman on the ground who will grab an unwary bird or monkey. There are also minor irritations. Vampire bats latch onto tapirs. They slice into their skin with razor-sharp teeth and lick the oozing blood. There is also a particularly irritating moth that sucks secretions from the corner of the tapir's eyes.

RAIN-FOREST GIANTS

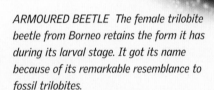

WHILE IT IS USUALLY THE MAMMALS AND BIRDS THAT STEAL THE LIMELIGHT (AND THE FOOD), there is an entire parallel world of rain-forest dwellers that are just as spectacular and equally important.
These are the invertebrates – animals without backbones – including worms, insects, spiders, centipedes and millipedes. Some have reached enormous proportions.

ARMOURED BEETLE The female trilobite beetle from Borneo retains the form it has during its larval stage. It got its name because of its remarkable resemblance to fossil trilobites.

VORACIOUS PREDATOR Some species of rain-forest centipede grow to a tremendous 30 cm long. They have vicious modified claws that deliver a potent venom to kill prey that can include mice, frogs and even bats.

Worms, centipedes and millipedes

On the forest floor of the Amazon rain forest, the job of recycling plant material falls in part to unusually large earthworms called sapana. These Amazon giants can reach 60 cm in length and have the diameter of a human thumb. They are rarely seen, emerging from the ground only after heavy rain has waterlogged the soil, or when marauding army ants pass through the forest. Earthworms are not confined to the forest floor. There are worms that live in the trees, breaking down organic debris there and recycling the soil that accumulates around epiphytes growing on the branches.

Earthworms in Borneo's Kinabalu Forest grow even larger, up to 70 cm long. They, too, appear only after rain, their blue-grey bodies glistening with a greenish iridescence caused by minute body hairs. They fall prey to the rare Kinabalu giant leech, a striking, bright orange-red leech that grows to 30 cm long. Unlike more familiar blood-sucking leeches, it feeds almost exclusively on the giant earthworms.

Brightly coloured Amazon flatworms, or planaria, can be up to 20 cm long. Little is know about their biology, but some species are thought to catch and eat terrestrial snails. Equally awesome are rain-forest centipedes, including the bright copper-red Peruvian giant centipede that grows to more than 30 cm long. This

HORNED BEETLE The horns on the head of the male rhinoceros beetle are like the antlers of a stag; they are not used to catch food but to fight rival males.

80 and 400 legs, but one very rare species from North America has 750. The largest is the giant African millipede which grows to 30 cm long. It lives amongst the leaf-litter on the rain-forest floor, and is mainly active at night.

Beetle mania

Rain-forest beetles grow to enormous sizes and each of the world's rain forests has its own giant. The male three-horned rhinoceros beetle of Borneo is the insect equivalent of the *Triceratops* – a dinosaur that had three distinctive facial horns. Similar giants in other forests are known variously as goliath, Hercules, elephant or stag beetles, but despite their impressive armoury, they are all vegetarians. Larval beetles feed on dead wood that has been infected with fungi, and adults feed on nectar, young leaves, sap and fruit. The fearsome appearance of these beetles, along with the loud hissing sound they emit when stressed, acts as an effective deterrent against many predators.

The title of world's largest beetle is generally given to the 17 cm long titan beetle of South America. Other contenders include the African goliath scarab beetle, which is shorter at 11 cm but bulkier, and the Hercules beetle of Central America, which has an enormously long horn and an overall length of about 18 cm. The brute strength of some of these insects is exceptional. While an elephant can lift a quarter of its own weight, the rhinoceros beetle can lift 850 times its own weight – the equivalent of a human lifting a small army tank. This makes them amongst the strongest animals on Earth – and it is all down to a meagre diet of rotting fruit and sap.

fast-moving carnivore kills its prey by injecting poison from large, modified claws, known as forcipules, which are located under the first body segment. It has been known to enter caves in Venezuelan forests and catch bats in mid-flight. More usually it catches insects and even other small mammals, such as mice. Its bite is extremely painful.

Giant millipedes, although harmless to people, exude hydrogen cyanide from glands along the length of the body when attacked. Some animals, such as capuchin monkeys in South America and lemurs in Madagascar, rub millipedes on their fur, probably to get rid of ticks and other external parasites. Millipedes are valuable members of the recycling party, eating decaying leaves and other dead plant material. None of them has a thousand legs. Depending on the species they have between

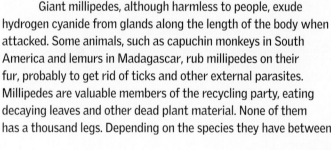

FOREST PREDAT

ORS5

THE RAIN FORESTS ARE PATROLLED BY SOME OF THE PLANET'S MOST POWERFUL EAGLES, SUCH AS THE PHILIPPINE MONKEY-EATING EAGLE (left). With so much food supporting such a great diversity of plant-eaters, it is not surprising that meat-eaters live in the forest, too. Large cats prowl the floor and understorey, while small cats climb into the canopy. These predators are secretive, agile and powerful, and their principle hunting strategy is stealth followed by a surprise attack, often over in the blink of an eye. Scientists sometimes refer to these hunters as 'indicator' species: if they are thriving, it is a sign that the rest of the forest is healthy. While many predators are large, some are tiny, such as driver and army ants. What they lack in size, they make up for by their numbers and a relentless ferocity that makes some larger animals flee in panic.

AERIAL PREDATORS

ALL OF THE WORLD'S MAJOR TRACTS OF RAIN FOREST HAVE a species of powerful eagle that patrols the skies above the canopy. South and Central America have the harpy eagle; South-east Asia has the Philippines monkey-eating eagle; and Africa has the crowned hawk-eagle. They are among the rain forest's top predators and their primary targets are monkeys.

Ferocious hunter

Named after the Harpies of Greek mythology, often portrayed with eagles' wings and talons, the harpy eagle of the Amazon rain forests is one of the world's most aggressive and powerful eagles. For its size it has short wings – the female has a 5.6 m wingspan –

EAGLE POWER A harpy eagle uses its formidable bill to slice up a rabbit. Its food can include sloths, monkeys, opossums and iguanas. It plucks a victim from a branch, sometimes flying upside down momentarily to snatch prey hanging down below the branch.

and a relatively long tail for manoeuvrability. Its foot spans 25 cm with 4 cm claws – similar in size to a grizzly bear's. These can pierce a monkey's brain and body, killing it instantly.

Harpy eagles nest in the highest emergent trees, and although the female (which is twice the size of the male) lays two eggs, only the first chick to hatch is reared by the parents; the other is ignored. The parents, which are life-long partners, hunt by day, catching small monkeys – about a third of their diet – as well as young sloths, opossums and coatis, and occasionally iguanas and birds. They watch and listen carefully to rain-forest sounds and when a troop of monkeys gives itself away, the bird launches itself after its prey at speeds in excess of 80 km/h.

Agile performer

The most powerful bird of prey in the Congo rain forest is the African crowned hawk-eagle. It has relatively short, rounded wings for dodging and weaving through the canopy. Each bird hunts a patch of forest about 10 km² and begins by soaring high above the canopy. When it sights a troop of monkeys, it settles

LOOKING BIGGER Like other rain-forest eagles, the crowned hawk-eagle has a crest of feathers which it raises when it is alert or showing hostility to an aggressor. Mammals make up about 98 per cent of the eagle's food – a child's skull has even been found in a nest.

some distance away. It edges ever closer, until it zips out and grabs a monkey – even one in mid-leap – then carries it vertically upwards to a perch, or back to its nest in the fork of an emergent tree. It will also take small antelope, such as duikers; less often it catches birds and lizards.

Eastern eagles

The island of New Guinea has its own harpy eagle, also known as the kapul eagle. Like its New World namesake, it flies above the forest canopy, but does not soar like other eagles. It is smaller than the South American harpy, but at 90 cm long, it is the largest non-human predator on the island. It catches ringtail possums, cuscuses, giant rats, wallabies, lizards, snakes, birds, small pigs and small dogs, often in an unusual way. It can run along the ground, climb trees and dash along branches to extract prey from tree hollows with its talons. At dawn and dusk it makes a resonant, low-frequency call, resembling a 'gulp'.

One of the world's rarest birds, and one of the largest eagles, is the Philippine eagle – about 1 m long with a wingspan of 5.6 m, similar to the South American harpy. Although known as a monkey-eating eagle, it feeds mainly on colugos, a kind of flying lemur. It will also take civets, large snakes, monitor lizards, small deer and birds, such as hornbills; dietary preferences depend on the fauna of each invididual island in the group. The Philippine eagle nests 30 m high in emergent trees, mainly dipterocarps.

TERRESTRIAL
PREDATORS

IN LINE WITH RAIN-FOREST HERBIVORES, WHICH TEND TO BE SMALLER THAN THEIR COUNTERPARTS ON THE SAVANNAH, most rain-forest predators tend to be smaller, too. The exceptions to this rule, such as the jaguar, have adapted to conditions in the forest – including the availability of prey – by hunting not only on the ground, but also in the trees.

Tiger, tiger

Many of the principal terrestrial predators are wild cats, and all the world's major rain forests, with the exception of those in Australasia, have their own dedicated feline hunters. The largest

SNAKE-CATCHER A South American ocelot takes a plunge to catch a young anaconda. It has good vision, including excellent night sight, but usually finds food by following the odour trail the prey has left behind.

rain-forest cat is the tiger, and several subspecies are found across southern Asia. They hunt the largest prey, such as deer and wild pigs. Their technique is first to stalk, then to rush their target at the last minute. The tiger has powerful hindquarters that enable it to leap onto its victim's back to bring it down – it can jump to a height of 5 m and as far as 9 m. A tiger will

AUSTRALIAN KILLER A spotted-tail quoll is a large carnivorous marsupial, extremely agile and at home in the canopy. Here, it has caught a parrot, but more often it takes marsupial mice, possums and bandicoots. It kills its victim by biting behind the head.

bite the neck of larger prey to constrict the windpipe and cause suffocation; with a smaller animal, it breaks the creature's neck.

About 80 per cent of tigers in the wild are Bengal tigers, living in the forests of the Indian subcontinent, but several southern Asian locations have their own subspecies. The Malaysian tiger inhabits the forests of the southern part of the Malay Peninsula. Thailand, Vietnam, Cambodia and Laos are home to the Indochinese tiger, and the island of Sumatra has the Sumatran tiger, the smallest subspecies. Balinese and Javan tigers are now extinct, and the other subspecies are greatly endangered due to habitat destruction and hunting for their fur and for body parts which are used in Chinese medicine.

Island cats

The clouded leopard is a medium-sized wild cat, just over 1 m long, found throughout southern Asia. It is famous for its beautiful coat, to which it owes its name, from the 'cloud' patterns on its fur. The islands of Borneo and Sumatra have their own subspecies, typified by darker fur and smaller 'clouds'. Its tail is almost as long as its body, and it has the longest canine teeth of any cat. Relatively short legs, large paws and sharp claws are adaptations to help it to climb trees and walk through thick forest. The clouded leopard can also walk upside down, hanging under a branch, and descend a tree head downwards. Little is known about its behaviour in the wild, but gibbons, macaques and proboscis monkeys are all known to fall prey.

Borneo also has the elusive and extremely rare bay cat, which is found only on the island. Fully grown, the bay cat reaches about 55 cm long, with a 35 cm tail. It has chestnut-coloured fur with white dots on the insides of the legs. It probably hunts small mammals and birds, but little is known about its behaviour. Most scientific data comes from museum specimens, and few people have seen it alive. Mainland cats, such as the marbled cat and leopard cat, are also found in Borneo, the latter being one of the smallest wild cats in the world.

Africa's top predator

In African rain forests, the leopard reigns supreme. It is widely distributed across the continent (and also in Asia), but is nocturnal and therefore rarely seen. While savannah leopards have been well studied, little is known about the habits of those that live in the rain forest, except that like all the rain-forest cats

AMERICAN CAT Pumas hunt in the rain forest, but are wary of the more powerful jaguar. Their home ranges overlap, but jaguars tend to take larger prey, such as capybaras, while pumas take medium-sized prey, such as collared peccaries.

they use stealth to approach their targets. They then spring a surprise attack to bring prey down.

A very dark-furred leopard, called the black panther, is sometimes seen in the rain forests of both Africa and Malaysia, accounting for half of all leopard sightings in the Malay Peninsula. It is not a separate species but simply a colour variation – or 'melanistic variant' – of the leopard. The leopard's more familiar pattern of whorls and spots can be seen faintly on the dark coat.

Amazon cats

The jaguar and the puma are the largest of the New World cats. Forest jaguars are darker than their swamp-living relatives, but all have a pattern of rosettes on the body. As with the leopard, some jaguars – about 6 per cent of the total population – are almost black. There are also extremely rare white (albino) jaguars. Aside from mothers with cubs, jaguars are generally solitary, males patrolling a territory of about 130 km² and females one-half that size. Ranges overlap and individuals declare their occupancy with loud, repetitive, cough-like roars.

The puma, also called the cougar, is found across North and South America, from the Yukon in Canada to the southern Andes. It is slightly smaller than the jaguar, with a tawny coat and long hind legs that make it an agile leaper and sprinter. In the rain-forest share-out between pumas and jaguars, the latter tend to take the larger prey. As a result, pumas in jaguar country tend to be smaller than those in other areas.

The South American rain forests are also home to several smaller species. The ocelot is about 1 m long, with a 45 cm tail. Its fur resembles that of the jaguar, but this cat is smaller and it has more delicate features. Resting by day and active by night, the ocelot is hard to see, for its

camouflaged coat makes it almost invisible. It is a good climber, but also stakes out the forest floor. Young deer, peccaries, monkeys, bats, sloths, coatis, agoutis and pacas are its main prey, but it will also catch birds, which it rushes rather than stalks.

The margay and the oncilla are close relatives of the ocelot. The margay is similar in size, but it is a more skilful climber and spends much more of its life in the trees, where it hunts at night, chasing birds and monkeys. Like the clouded leopard, the margay can come down a tree head first. The oncilla, a nocturnal hunter with a spotted coat, is smaller than the margay – slightly larger than a domestic cat.

The jaguarondi is a New World cat without spots, more closely related to the puma. With brownish-grey fur, it resembles an otter more than a cat. It climbs but more usually hunts on the ground where it catches small reptiles, mammals, birds and fish.

No-feline zone

In Australia's cat-free rain forests the top predator niche is occupied by a carnivorous marsupial, the spotted-tail quoll. It has chestnut-coloured fur with large white spots and looks a bit like a long domestic cat, with shorter legs. It moves in bounds, climbs well and hunts for various prey, from insects to mammals, such as small wallabies. It is solitary and nocturnal. A key feature is its yawning gape. When threatened, the quoll lets out a piercing scream – once heard, it is said, the cry is never forgotten.

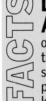

LEOPARDS HAVE BEEN RECORDED AS EATING UP TO 90 SPECIES of animal, from dung beetles to large antelopes. Sometimes, their diet includes humans. A famous 'man-eater' was the so-called Panar Leopard, said to have killed and eaten 400 people in the Kumaon district in northern India. A well-known big cat hunter, Jim Corbett, shot it in 1910.

BENGAL TIGERS in the Sundarbans forests of Bangladesh stalk and sometimes kill people that enter the forests to collect honey or firewood.

CLOUDED LEOPARDS ARE AS AGILE AS SQUIRRELS in trees They are active both day and night.

JAGUAR

ONE OF THE WORLD'S FOUR

'BIG CATS', THE JAGUAR IS THE TOP PREDATOR IN THE NEW WORLD RAIN FORESTS AND THE LARGEST, MOST POWERFUL CAT IN THE WESTERN HEMISPHERE. With a bite more damaging than that of any other cat, it can pierce the head of a victim, such as a capybara, and crush the brain inside the skull and can slice through a turtle's carapace in one bite. It inhabits dense jungle, especially in areas close to water, and open swamp regions, such as the Pantanal of western Brazil. It often goes swimming and is as at home in the trees as on the ground. When stalking prey, a jaguar moves ever nearer until close enough to make a sudden dash and pounce, usually from behind, in the victim's blind spot. It hunts mainly at dawn and dusk, taking tapirs, peccaries, deer and pacas on the ground, and sloths, monkeys and birds in the trees. It also fishes and digs for river turtle eggs. A jaguar will tackle giants, such as anacondas and caiman, but it also takes small creatures, such as mice and frogs. It can haul a large carcass, even a cow, up a tree or swimming.

CLASS: Mammalia
ORDER: Carnivora
SPECIES: *Panthera onca*
HABITAT: Tropical forests
DISTRIBUTION: South and Central America
KEY FEATURES: Powerful jaws and an ability to climb trees

VITAL STATISTICS

PREDATORY ANTS

BY FAR THE MOST NUMEROUS AND SUCCESSFUL PREDATORS IN THE RAIN FOREST ARE ANTS. With tens of millions in a single colony, they can overcome creatures much bigger than themselves.

Working together, they form a super-organism, coordinated by a complex system of smells and vibrations. Ants will also fight other ants. In the Amazon, aggressive Azteca ants use chemical sprays to beat off more lightly armed crazy ants, and fire ants spray food with noxious chemicals to ward off rivals. The most impressive species of all are the driver ants of the Old World and the army ants of the New World.

Raiding driver ants

Also known as siafu, driver ants live in African rain forests. They kill every living thing they can pin down, from scorpions and cockroaches to chickens and cows. The ant swarm raids on a broad front up to 15 m across, moving like a black tide at 20 m an hour. On contact with prey, the ant emits a chemical that recruits other ants to help. In seconds, their victim is smothered, sliced up and carried back to the nest along well-used trails. They might catch, kill and transport 100 000 victims in one day.

The nest or bivouac is a temporary home. The walls and corridors are made entirely of living ants with their legs linked together. At the centre of the nest is the queen – at 5 cm long the world's largest ant – who produces 1 to 2 million eggs a month. The workers are not divided into castes, but vary in size from the smallest 'nursemaids', which look after the eggs and larvae, to the largest 'soldiers', which guard the foraging trails. In between are workers that kill, slice and carry, and the winged males that do very little until breeding time.

A single colony can contain up to 22 million ants, most of them sisters. It is the largest family on Earth. All are blind, finding their way about by following chemical highways on the ground and relying on touch and vibrations to attack prey. The swarm raids until the patch of forest is empty and then the colony moves on, travelling along avenues lined by guards. Workers carry the eggs, larvae and pupae and escort the queen to a new bivouac site. From this base, they start raiding all over again.

Army ants in procession

South and Central American rain forests are home to army ants, which can be either swarm raiders or column raiders, depending on the species. Almost blind, they also rely on chemicals for communication and finding their way about. They feed mainly on insects, spiders and scorpions on the ground, and raid termite and wasp nests in the trees.

An entire procession of other creatures follows army ants, pouncing on insects the ants have flushed out. Antbirds position themselves close to the swarm front, in line with the pecking order of the species. Large birds take prime positions ahead of the ants, while smaller species, such as the spotted antbird, spread out on either side. A mixed flock of other species follows close behind. Antshrikes are the sentinels, warning all the other birds of approaching danger.

Ant butterflies follow the army, too, and take minerals from the nitrogen-rich antbird droppings. Other insects live within the ant network. Silverfish, ant-mimicking beetles, solitary wasps and millipedes disguise themselves with the right kind of smells and live right inside the ant bivouac. Local people even allow army ants into their homes to get rid of household nests – they are the ultimate natural pest controllers.

BIG SISTER The African driver ant soldier has enormous jaws with which it protects the colony, but it is incapable of feeding itself. Smaller ants supply it with liquid food which is passed mouth-to-mouth.

INSECT-EATING SPECIALISTS

THE EXTRAORDINARY NUMBERS OF ANTS AND TERMITES MAKE THEM ONE OF THE RAIN FORESTS' LARGEST FOOD RESOURCES. Anteaters, found in all the world's major rain forests, have evolved precisely to exploit this resource. It is not the easiest of niches to occupy. The anteaters' tiny prey have formidable weapons in the form of powerful razor-sharp jaws, noxious secretions and fiery, burning stings. And there are so many of them in a colony, any creature not adapted to the task would be overwhelmed in minutes. In order to feed on such difficult and dangerous prey, each of the rain-forest anteaters has its own form of protection from the bites and stings, and specially adapted jaws and tongues to eat the prey .

ALL-OVER ARMOUR The long-tailed pangolin from the Congo has an impregnable suit of armour. Its tail is partially prehensile – adapted to seize hold of branches – with a sensitive bare patch on the underside that helps it climb through the trees. Pangolins can also walk upright on two legs, using the tail for balance.

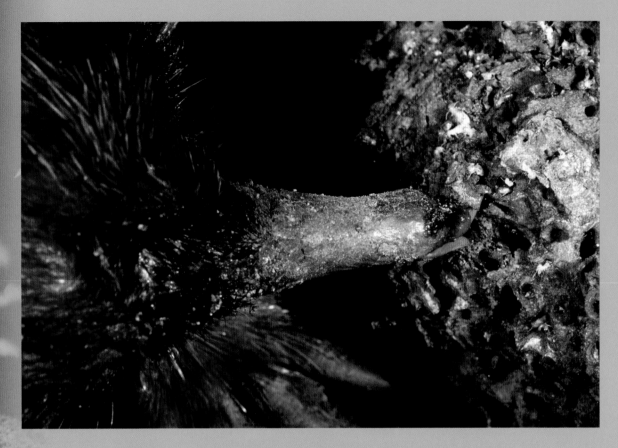

PRICKLY EGG-LAYER The echidna has an especially good sense of smell and a long snout to probe for ants and termites. Its long, flexible tongue can extend up to 18 cm from the tip of its snout. When feeding, it moves its tongue in and out in rapid flicks.

Walking brush

The giant anteater or ant bear is the world's largest anteater, found in the Amazon rain forest and on adjoining grasslands, where it feeds mainly on termites. It is one of the strangest-looking animals on Earth. Up to 1.3 m long, it has a long, narrow head, heavy-duty claws on short, stout legs, and a 9 cm long brush-like tail. Having poor vision, the giant anteater relies on a keen sense of smell to locate inhabited mounds. It then digs a hole in the nest with its large front claws and pushes in its very long tongue, licking up termites at a rate of 150 licks per minute and consuming in excess of 30 000 termites or ants in a day. It has no teeth, but grinds the insects, using hard growths in its mouth and sand and pebbles in its muscular stomach.

While the giant anteater forages on the ground, there are three smaller New World anteaters that find their food in the trees. The northern and southern tamanduas have partially prehensile tails for a life in the canopy, where they feed on ants, termites and sometimes bees. The silky anteater is even smaller, with a length, including its tail, of 45 cm. It has soft, golden fur, a partially prehensile tail and large front claws.

Pangolins or scaly anteaters inhabit African and Asian rain forests. There are eight species ranging in size from 30 cm to 100 cm long, and they are recognised by the armoured scales all over the body. These are made of keratin, the same material as human fingernails. The scales' razor-sharp edges protect the pangolin not only from ants and termites, but also potential predators. When it curls into a ball, with its face tucked under its tail, it becomes almost impregnable. For added safety, the pangolin can spray a noxious chemical from glands at the rear of its body, much like a skunk. Foraging at night, it has powerful front claws for digging into anthills and termite mounds and a sticky tongue – up to 60 cm long – to mop up the inmates.

Spiny ant-eating

The rain forests of Queensland and Papua New Guinea have their own kind of anteater – the echidna or spiny anteater. It is a monotreme, a mammal that lays eggs. It is solitary and mainly active at dawn and dusk. There are four species, each covered in hair and spines, making them look like hedgehogs. A long, slender snout functions as nose and mouth, and large claws on the forefeet are adapted for breaking into ants' and termite nests. Like the other anteaters, echidnas have long sticky tongues to lick up their prey. Their long snouts can also be used as snorkels when crossing rivers. If danger threatens, an echidna digs down rapidly on soft soil and erects its spines so that all that can be seen is its spiny back. If it is on hard ground, it simply rolls into a ball.

RAIN-FOREST SPIDERS

THE RAIN FORESTS BRIM WITH SPIDERS, ALL FEASTING ON THE PLENTIFUL SUPPLY OF FOOD. Some trap their prey in elaborate webs; others, such as the huntsman spiders of South-east Asia and Queensland, chase it on the ground or in the trees. Instead of weaving webs, huntsman spiders wait in tree crevices for insects to go by. When one comes close, the huntsman sets off in pursuit. It can crawl sideways on long, crab-like legs; one species in Laos has a leg span of 30 cm.

Golden orb-web spiders are the largest species to construct complex webs. They are found in many of the world's rain forests, the female more evident than the male, as she is so much larger. Although her body is decorated with blacks and yellows, it is the golden hue of her web that gives this spider its name. The web can be huge, up to 6 m high and 2 m wide. Birds sometimes get trapped in its strong silk, but as insects, not birds, form the spider's diet, this is not a welcome catch. The spider weaves special

FAST SPIDER The huntsman spider catches prey by chasing it down. It also has a 'cling reflex' so if it attaches to clothing it is difficult to pull off, much to the consternation of humans who are not keen on spiders.

lines of silk into the web, like a large cross, to warn birds of the obstruction. The web may remain in place for several years.

Most spiders are solitary, but in the Amazon there are some that live together and work as a team. Of the 20 or so known species of social spider, one of the most gregarious is a *Theridion* spider found in Ecuador. Several thousand individuals sometimes live together, although more usually there are just a few dozen in smaller nests. They trap prey by hanging threads of sticky silk from leaves and branches, then wait until a careless insect flies into the strands. It is ensnared just long enough for a posse of spiders to throw a net of silk webbing over it. They paralyse the prey with venom from their tiny jaws and carry it back to the communal nest, where it is shared with the rest of the colony.

The spider with the largest web is another Ecuadorian species, from the genus *Anelosimus*. The largest, hammock-

SOCIAL SPIDER Anelosimus *spiders build huge webs in which several generations may live together. Only a few spiders immobilise any prey trapped in the web, but many share the food when it has been caught. Most are females – the males appear only at breeding time.*

shaped webs are about 7.6 m long and 2.4 m wide. They are home to more than 50 000 mahogany-coloured spiders, which are truly social. The colony splits up only when the web becomes too large to remain in one piece. Several groups of spider head out into the forest and start the web-building all over again.

In the African rain forests, the small, striped *Agelena* spider builds a system of horizontal webs joined by vertical filaments. Flying insects blunder into these strands and drop into the hammock below or are herded down by the spiders. Females capture prey, while smaller spiders maintain the web

MEALS OF BLOOD

ALL OVER THE WORLD, ANIMALS HAVE DISCOVERED THE NUTRITIONAL ADVANTAGES OF FEEDING ON THE BLOOD OF OTHERS. The rain forests are no exception – they have leeches, vampire bats, flies, midges and mosquitoes.

In the Amazon's flooded forests – the areas inundated during the river's annual floods (see page 140) – the mosquito population increases dramatically as the water level rises. The insects' aquatic larvae grow in the flood waters, but there is less land on which the females' mammalian prey can be found. As a result, any warm-blooded creature in the forest after dark comes under relentless attack. People sometimes have to stop talking in case they get a mouthful of insects. In places, the inhabitants finish their chores at 6.25 pm and head for their mosquito nets. Exactly five minutes later every female mosquito is on the search for a blood meal.

Forest suckers

Rain-forest leeches are unlike other leech species. They tend not to live in water, but are adapted to the humid conditions in a tropical forest. They do not feed frequently, but wait, sometimes for months, for animals to chance by. They have sensors that pick up the body heat, vibration, movement and carbon dioxide given off by warm-blooded prey. They drop from branches or climb up legs, and the victim rarely feels their bites. The leeches have razor-sharp teeth and produce an anaesthetic to numb the incision and an anticoagulant to make the blood flow freely. They might consume as much as 15 times their own body weight in blood, enough to keep them going until the next blood meal – maybe six to 12 months away.

Vampires in the night

On the darkest nights, mammals and birds living on the floor and in the understorey of the rain forests of South and Central America are confronted by an unusual hunter – the vampire bat. There are three species, two feeding mainly on bird blood and one favouring mammals, including humans.

Vampires take to the wing on moonless nights in order to avoid predators and to approach victims without being seen. The bat lands some distance from its target, then crawls towards it along the ground, supported by its leathery wings and short legs. Two pads on its face act as infrared sensors, which detect the warmth of blood vessels close to the victim's skin, indicating the best places to bite. The bat makes an 8 mm deep incision with chisel-like incisor teeth and then injects saliva containing anticoagulants to stop the blood from clotting and blood vessels from constricting. With its grooved tongue, the bat licks, rather than sucks, the blood flowing from the wound.

BLOODSUCKER The tiger leech of South-east Asia and Australasia is just 2 cm long. With a sucker at its rear end, it attaches itself to a leaf, leaving the sucker at the front end ready to attach to prey. It detects prey partly by the carbon dioxide the victim gives off, and it can sense movement.

BLOOD-LICKER A vampire bat uses its grooved tongue to lick blood from a cow's leg. The cow will probably not have noticed that it is donating blood. The bat clipped away any hair and then made a delicate incision. It might feed for 30 minutes before the cow wakes up.

The vampire makes a hearty meal of blood. The creature itself weighs about 40 g, but during the 20 or so minutes that it feeds, it will consume as much as 20 g of blood before it is sated. Under normal circumstances, this would make it extremely difficult for the bat to take off, but it digests the blood rapidly. Within two minutes of starting to feed, it is pumping out urine containing diluted blood fluids, having absorbed most of the useful nutrients.

Animals attacked by vampires in the wild are rarely injured or killed, but tethered domestic stock can be weakened considerably by repeated visits. Vampires themselves become weak if they cannot get blood. They need to feed every couple of days, and if they fail, they can beg for blood from other more successful bats returning to the roost. The blood transfusion is given mouth-to-mouth. Despite their sinister reputation vampire bats are caring, sharing animals. They will even adopt and feed orphaned youngsters.

Deadly assassins

The insects called true bugs or hemipterans, which include aphids and cicadas, have mouthparts that are like hypodermic needles. In most species, these are to suck sap from plant stems, but a few have adapted their stabbing habit to drink the blood and other body fluids of animals. One is the assassin bug, which ambushes insects. The forelegs of some assassin bug species are smeared with resins and held out in front of the bug; others have spiny pads on their front appendages. Inquisitive insects are trapped in the resin or impaled on the spines and are then injected with chemicals that dissolve the victim's insides. The bug then sucks them dry. One species uses the dried out skins of termites to attract other termites, like an angler with a lure.

LIVING TOGETHER

6

WORKING ALONE MEANS AN ANIMAL NEED NOT SHARE ITS FOOD OR LIVING SPACE, BUT THERE ARE ADVANTAGES IN POOLING RESOURCES. Large numbers of animals, such as insects, can work together selflessly for the greater good of the colony, to the benefit of individuals as well as the group. Successful cohabitation also occurs among animals or plants of different species. An association where both partners benefit is generally known as 'symbiosis'. If one of the partners takes advantage of the other to the extent that one is harmed, it is called 'parasitism'. Both strategies can be observed in the rain forest, with some unexpected outcomes. The strawberry poison-dart frog (left) is dependent on rainwater pools in bromeliad plants to rear its tadpoles. The frog feeds the tadpoles unfertilised eggs and the plant absorbs any leftovers.

COLONIES

THE RAIN FOREST IS HOME TO A WIDE ARRAY OF COLONIES, FROM THE ROOSTS of fruit bats found high in rain-forest trees, to mud mounds of social insects living on the forest floor. The social insects include wasps, bees, ants and termites and they form some of the biggest colonies on Earth. Some are predators, others farmers, and some scavengers.

Farmer ants

Leafcutter ants have developed a sophisticated system of agriculture, which begins in the canopy where they cut leaves with their scissor-like mandibles. They carry the leaf pieces back to their underground nests along extensive trails that wind through the rain forest. The ants take the freshly cut leaves below ground to special football-sized chambers – not to eat them, but to turn them into compost to cultivate a particular type of fungus. The ants and the fungus have a symbiotic relationship. The ants bring in the right kind of leaves for the fungus to grow, and the fungus rewards them by producing special nutrient-rich structures called gongylidia that grow on the fungal threads. These are the ants' main food supply, which

they also feed to their larvae. A bacterium that grows on the ants' bodies produces chemicals that help to protect the fungus against the growth of harmful moulds.

A leafcutter colony contains upwards of 8 million ants. There are four castes, each with a different role. The smallest, minims, tend the brood and 'weed' the fungus gardens. The minors patrol the foraging columns, attacking any predators, while the mediae cut and carry the leaf fragments back to the nest. The largest of the worker leafcutters are the majors, who help defend the nest against intruders such as army ants.

The greatest threat to the ant columns is a tiny parasitic phorid fly that lays its eggs in an ant's head. The ants have a defence: tiny minim workers ride shotgun on the leaves carried by the mediae workers to ward off any attack.

Sweat bees

A walk in the rain forest can bring unwanted attention from trigonid bees – small dark bees that more closely resemble flies. Some species are stingless and generally collect nectar from flowers, but if an unfortunate perspiring human chances by, they home in on the sweat to take advantage of the useful

PAPER HOME Paper wasps scrape wood from the bark of rain-forest trees and mix it with saliva to form a wood pulp. This malleable material is then used to construct a waterproof nest. Eggs are laid singly in the hexagonal cells. Mature nests contain up to 200 cells.

minerals it contains. Trigonid bees are found in most rain forests, where they make wax nests in tree hollows. The nests in South-east Asia are often built defensively, with funnel-shaped entrances that the bees seal up at night to prevent predators making a surprise attack.

In the Amazon, a species of trigonid bee has adopted a slightly different lifestyle: it has become a scavenger akin to a vulture. It specialises in cutting into and feeding on the carcasses of animals, such as dead frogs. The bee operates alongside a scavenger species of *Crematogaster* ant, and the two species have come to an agreement: the ants have access to the meal by day and the bees at night.

Another species of trigonid bee, this time with a sting in its tail, enjoys a close relationship both with a bird and with termites. The bird is the oropendola, a species that builds bag-like nests that hang from branches high in the canopy. While the nesting chicks are safe from predators such as emerald tree boas, they are still vulnerable to attack by hornbills. So the birds build their nests in close proximity to colonies of the stinging bees. The bees seem to recognise the birds as neighbours – probably by smell – and leave them alone, but they will fiercely

attack any other intruders. The bees for their part are often troubled by predatory wasps and ants, which the oropendolas catch, so there is a mutual advantage in the two species living close together.

The bees gain further protection by building their nests in termite mounds, where soldier termites mount an effective guard. The termites tolerate the bees because they harass tamanduas and other tree-living insect-eaters.

Weaver ants

Australian forests are home to colonies of the Queensland green tree ant – one of the weaver ants, a group found in most tropical rain forests. They live in trees and build – or weave – their nests entirely from leaves in a highly unique way. Groups of workers line up along the edges of leaves, like a chain gang, and pull them together. While they hold the leaves tight, other workers use silk produced by their larvae to 'glue' the edges together. The finished nests are roughly oval shaped and can be up to 50 cm long.

There may be as many as 150 nests in a single colony that spans several trees. A colony may house a single queen whose eggs are distributed between the many satellite nests, or there may be several queens living in a complex society. Whatever the system, there can be 100 000 to 500 000 ants at home. And they are extremely aggressive. They will defend their nests vigorously, grabbing an intruder with their sharp mandibles. They then squirt formic acid from the tip of their abdomen into their opponent's wound.

LIVING GLUE In the Queensland rain forest, green ants construct their nests from leaves glued together with silk produced by their larvae. The tree benefits because the ants attack other insects that would eat the leaves.

Termite towers

Although they are sometimes called 'white ants', termites are not ants at all, but colonial cockroaches. They are part of the recycling system of the rain forest, feeding primarily on the cellulose in dead plant material and rotting wood, which is broken down by 'friendly' bacteria and other symbiotic microorganisms in the termite's gut. They collect food from the forest around the nest. While foraging they hide amongst the vegetation or in the soil so they are rarely seen. Their foraging area might cover a hectare of rain forest, their runways or galleries extending as much as 50 m from the colony.

Termite nests are constructed of dried mud and saliva that harden like concrete. The shape varies with the species. Some nests can be a towering 7 m high, although most rain-forest species tend to build smaller mounds. Some are shaped like a mushroom, the cap helping to keep the rain from washing away the rest of the nest, and others have frilly skirt-like projections, like tiles on a roof, for the same purpose. The termite mound serves as an almost impregnable castle of clay to keep out predators. Should an intruder happen to get past this first line of defence, however, there is an altogether nastier deterrent waiting in the wings.

Most termite species have a large and fearsome soldier caste, equipped with all manner of weapons depending on the species. Many have enormous and powerful mandibles. One species has a nozzle on its head through which it squirts sticky, noxious substances to incapacitate an aggressor and another has a brush on its face primed with toxic chemicals. Whatever the species, the soldiers tend to be heavily armoured, sterile and blind, and their heads have become so specialised that they cannot feed themselves. They rely on liquid foods fed to them by other smaller members of the colony. Some simply use their solidly built heads to block entrances and corridors in the termite mound should smaller predators, such as driver ants, infiltrate the colony.

At the centre of the colony is the queen, an enormous sausage-like egg-laying machine, who can live for up to 50 years. She is the reason for the colony's existence and all its activities are geared up to one thing: keeping the queen safe and healthy so she can produce the offspring that enables the colony to continue. The queen keeps herself busy – laying one egg every ten to 15 seconds of her life.

Termites can be so numerous that a square metre of tropical rain forest soil might contain more than 10 000 termites and in some forests they can represent 98 per cent of the weight of insects present. There are over 2600 living species, and they can be divided generally into the 'lower' termites that have a symbiotic relationship with bacteria and protozoans to break down wood, and the higher termites, which feed on a variety of plant materials. Like leafcutter ants, some species of higher termites are farmers. Instead of leaves, however, they return to the nest with decaying wood on which they grow a special type of fungus.

CEMENT TOWER A termite mound houses millions of termites. The tiny insects are good for the forest as they recycle decaying material. They also provide food for frogs, lizards, birds and anteaters.

TITAN ARUM

THE FLOWERHEAD OF THE TITAN ARUM IS ONE OF THE LARGEST AND MOST UNUSUAL FLOWERS IN THE WORLD, WITH A MOST UNAPPEALING PERFUME.

It grows naturally only on the island of Sumatra, although it can be found in many botanical gardens throughout the world, where every time it flowers it causes a sensation. The inflorescence stands about 3 m tall and, like its smaller relative the cuckoo spit or arum lily, it consists of a long spadix with both male and female flowers wrapped in a spathe that resembles a huge single petal. Apart from its size, the titan arum's most remarkable characteristic is its smell. It is often called the 'carrion flower' or 'corpse plant' on account of the overwhelming aroma of rotting meat – a scent that attracts sweat bees to pollinate it. The stench is produced when the spadix reaches human body temperature, the warmth helping to vaporise the odour. The smell peaks in intensity on two consecutive evenings, once when the pink female flowers open, and then again when the cream-coloured male flowers produce pollen. This timing reduces the chance of self-pollination. Insects attracted to the plant on the first day enter the female flowers at the base of the spadix and any pollen they are carrying from another plant is brushed onto the female flowers. The pollinators become trapped until the male flowers have shed their pollen the following day. The spathe then withers enough to allow the insects with their fresh dusting of pollen to fly off in search of another smelly flower. The plants do not grow close to one another, so the large inflorescence is thought to help to disperse the evil-smelling scent over a wide area.

VITAL STATISTICS

CLASS: Liliopsida

ORDER: Alismatales

SPECIES: *Amorphophallus titanum*

HABITAT: Tropical rain forests of Sumatra

KEY FEATURE: Enormous inflorescence that emits a powerful scent of rotting flesh.

MOST PLANT AND INSECT INTERACTIONS ARE
LOOSELY COORDINATED. Bees and other flying
insects visit flowers to take nectar and
inadvertently carry pollen from one flower
to another. The species of insect and the species of
flower are immaterial; each takes advantage of the other
regardless of who or what they are. But some species have
forged such a close, mutually dependent relationship that,
over millions of years, they have come to rely on each other
for protection and reproduction.

The wasp that does care a fig

For every species of fig tree in the Congo rain forest, there is an
equivalent fig wasp. The wasps and figs have co-evolved over
millions of years and they are so dependent on one another that their
life cycles are entwined. The female wasp, no more than a millimetre
long, flies great distances through the forest searching for fig trees in
flower. Only a few out of many thousands make it.

When the wasp finds the correct species, it enters the flower
by a small hole at one end – the ostiole – but its journey is not yet over.
It has to push its way down a tube that is lined by tightly closed
bracts. The female's body is flattened and there are special teeth on
the underside of its head and on its legs that help it squeeze through.
The fit is so tight that the wasp's antennae and wings break off. Inside,
the wasp finds an inward-facing flower that is designed especially for
this visit. It lays about 300 eggs and then dies. The eggs hatch
into wingless males and winged females, which mate with
one another. The males chew an exit hole through which
the winged females escape and then the males die, having never left

STRANGE PARTNERSHIPS

*EGG-LAYING TUBE The exceptionally
long ovipositor of the torymid fig wasp
enables her to place her eggs inside the
flower-bearing structure of the fig while
she remains on the outside.*

ANT FOOD In the Amazon rain forest of Peru, the Cecropia *tree grows special food bodies, rich in fats and proteins, for its Azteca ant residents. In return, the ants protect the tree from insects that would otherwise graze on its leaves.*

the confines of the flower. At about the same time, the fig flower produces pollen, which the female wasp gathers into a special receptacle on its body. It then leaves the flower and goes in search of another fig flower which it then enters, thus carrying pollen from one flower to another.

There are also non-pollinating fig wasps – about 30 different species for each species of fig tree. One type of winged female sneaks in with the pollinating wasp and lays its eggs. Others have a long egg-laying probe, called an ovipositor, which is pushed through the fig wall. These 'non-pollinators' bring nothing to the relationship, but simply take advantage of the life cycles of the two dependent species.

The ant-protection squad

In the Amazon rain forest, the umbrella or trumpet tree (*Cecropia*) is a 'pioneer' species, growing quickly in places where rain-forest giants have crashed down or in other clearings, and providing the ground cover necessary for the survival of less-hardy plant species. The tree, which is always in danger of being weighed down with a tangle of vines and lianas, ensures that it is not too encumbered as it grows by playing host to some little helpers that keep the vegetation in check. These are Azteca ants and they prevent the growth of any stems that invade by snipping them off. Plant-eating insects are deterred from visiting and sap-sucking mealy bugs that tap into the plant's sugar transport system are 'milked' for the honeydew they exude. In return, the ants are given free accommodation – special compartments in the hollow stems of the tree. They feed from brown patches under the leaf stems that secrete oils and high-energy carbohydrates. This partnership ensures the plant remains healthy and free of vines and epiphytes, so it can grow unimpeded, while the ants have a safe home with a ready supply of food.

In the Congo, a similar relationship exists between the *Barteria* ant and the *Barteria* tree. The newly arrived queen ant cuts a hole in a branch and climbs inside where she finds a series of hollow chambers. Here she establishes a new colony, her offspring protected inside the hollows. They feed on sugary liquids 'milked' from tiny scale insects that tap into the tree's sap and from special food bodies produced by the tree. Like on the umbrella tree, the ants protect the *Barteria* tree from leaf-eaters, such as caterpillars. Any insects that alight on it are savagely attacked and driven away. The ants also destroy any butterfly or moth eggs they find and chisel away any moulds that grow on the leaves. The ants, however, are not the only insects to have noticed the tree's free hand out. Some wasps rob the ants. Two or three wasps keep the ants occupied at the entrance to their nest, while other wasps collect food bodies and carry them away.

Not all ant species are rewarded directly by their host tree. One species of stinging ant in the Amazon lives in hollows in the leaves of a shade-tolerant rain-forest tree, whose saplings survive in a suppressed state in the understorey. The ants repel any leaf-eating insect, such as caterpillars, but they do not eat their prey. Instead, they keep scale insects in their nest, which they 'milk' for the honeydew that they extract from the tree. The ants gain from the relationship because they obtain their main source of energy from the honeydew, and the tree gains because its leaves are protected. The payment it makes via the sap-sucking scale insects is negligible compared to the damage that might be done to its leaves by caterpillars and the like. When confined to the understorey for much of its life, every square centimetre of leaf area is vital for collecting energy from the little sunlight that filters down from above.

of Nepenthes albomarginata *lures the termites to their death.*

other flies, similarly immune to the digestive juices, feed on them. It is thought that the reason the ants are tolerated in this way is that they prevent the plant from overeating. If too many insects fell into the pitcher, they could putrefy and upset the plant's chemical balance of digestive juices. They could even bring about the untimely death of the pitcher. The ants prevent any binge eating, and are given free meals and nesting rights for their trouble.

Another pitcher plant *Nepenthes lowii* has adopted a novel way to obtain fertiliser. It has a wide mouth, much like a trumpet, and the pitcher is constricted in the middle. The pitcher attracts birds, rather than insects, to its rim with the offer of a sugary snack. The birds land on the lip, but the sugar-secreting glands are placed in such a way that in order to reach them the bird must turn its back on the opening of the pitcher. In this way, nitrogen-rich bird droppings fall straight down into the reservoir.

The pitcher of *Nepenthes rafflesiana* is the venue for a gladiatorial contest. The combatants are the aggressive aquatic larvae of gnats, which tend to be territorial, even in the teacup-sized pitcher, and fight to the death. The gnats are immune to the plant's secretions while they are alive, but when they die they are fair game and digested along with everything else.

Unlike the other pitchers that feed on anything that falls into their trap, the monkey's-rice-pot pitcher plant, *Nepenthes albomarginata,* is more fussy about what it eats. The top of the pitcher has a line of edible white hair-like projections which forest termites find irresistible. They flock to the pitcher in their tens and even hundreds. When they come to feed they slip and fall in at the rate of one every three seconds. After an hour, all the tiny hairs are gone so the termites lose interest and leave, while the plant is left with a pitcher full of food to digest.

As well as trapping insects, the purple pitcher plant *Sarracenia purpurea* houses a complete miniature ecosystem in its pitcher. There are aquatic mites and three species of fly maggot that feed on prey at the surface, a midge larva that tackles prey which has sunk to the bottom, a mosquito larva that eats particulate matter in the water column and a variety of bacteria that speed up the rapid breakdown of trapped corpses. The bacteria, together with the other creatures, help the pitcher

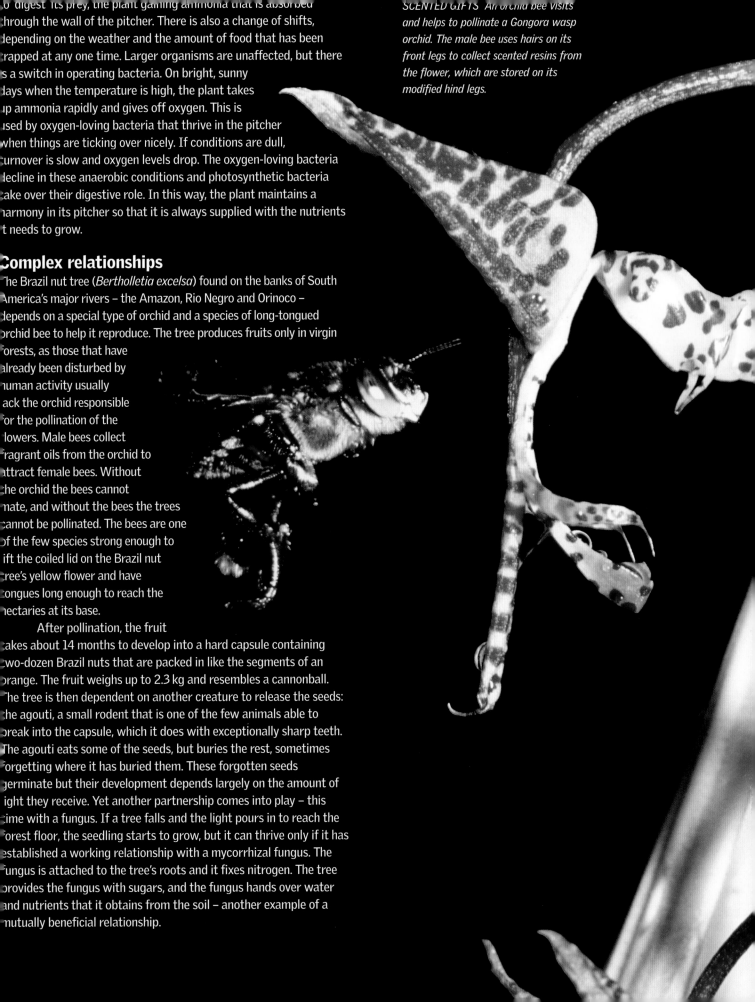

digest its prey, the plant gaining ammonia that is absorbed through the wall of the pitcher. There is also a change of shifts, depending on the weather and the amount of food that has been trapped at any one time. Larger organisms are unaffected, but there is a switch in operating bacteria. On bright, sunny days when the temperature is high, the plant takes up ammonia rapidly and gives off oxygen. This is used by oxygen-loving bacteria that thrive in the pitcher when things are ticking over nicely. If conditions are dull, turnover is slow and oxygen levels drop. The oxygen-loving bacteria decline in these anaerobic conditions and photosynthetic bacteria take over their digestive role. In this way, the plant maintains a harmony in its pitcher so that it is always supplied with the nutrients it needs to grow.

Complex relationships

The Brazil nut tree (*Bertholletia excelsa*) found on the banks of South America's major rivers – the Amazon, Rio Negro and Orinoco – depends on a special type of orchid and a species of long-tongued orchid bee to help it reproduce. The tree produces fruits only in virgin forests, as those that have already been disturbed by human activity usually lack the orchid responsible for the pollination of the flowers. Male bees collect fragrant oils from the orchid to attract female bees. Without the orchid the bees cannot mate, and without the bees the trees cannot be pollinated. The bees are one of the few species strong enough to lift the coiled lid on the Brazil nut tree's yellow flower and have tongues long enough to reach the nectaries at its base.

After pollination, the fruit takes about 14 months to develop into a hard capsule containing two-dozen Brazil nuts that are packed in like the segments of an orange. The fruit weighs up to 2.3 kg and resembles a cannonball. The tree is then dependent on another creature to release the seeds: the agouti, a small rodent that is one of the few animals able to break into the capsule, which it does with exceptionally sharp teeth. The agouti eats some of the seeds, but buries the rest, sometimes forgetting where it has buried them. These forgotten seeds germinate but their development depends largely on the amount of light they receive. Yet another partnership comes into play – this time with a fungus. If a tree falls and the light pours in to reach the forest floor, the seedling starts to grow, but it can thrive only if it has established a working relationship with a mycorrhizal fungus. The fungus is attached to the tree's roots and it fixes nitrogen. The tree provides the fungus with sugars, and the fungus hands over water and nutrients that it obtains from the soil – another example of a mutually beneficial relationship.

SCENTED GIFTS *An orchid bee visits and helps to pollinate a Gongora wasp orchid. The male bee uses hairs on its front legs to collect scented resins from the flower, which are stored on its modified hind legs.*

POOLS IN THE SKY

It has been estimated that at least 470 species of rain-forest animals live in or are closely associated with bromeliad pools.

MUCH OF THE HEAVY RAINFALL THAT LANDS ON THE RAIN-FOREST CANOPY IS RAPIDLY LOST THROUGH RUN-OFF OR EVAPORATION. Fortunately for the many animals that live there, an oasis can be found in a rain-forest plant – the bromeliad. These epiphytes growing on the branches of rain-forest trees collect water in pools or 'tanks' in their closely packed leaf whorls. Large specimens can contain up to 9 litres of water, and each pool is home to an entire ecosystem.

It has been estimated that at least 470 species live in or are closely associated with bromeliad tanks. Monkeys drink from them, frogs deposit their eggs in them and aquatic insect larvae live in them. The larvae of some species of midge, mosquito, dragonfly and mayfly depend on them totally. A species of bladderwort grows in the pool, and it catches aquatic insect larvae with the help of tiny bladders.

The bromeliads themselves benefit from their visitors. Blue-green algae fix nitrogen that is absorbed through the walls of the plant's tank, although some bromeliads have taken things too far – like pitcher plants, they secrete enzymes into the water and digest the inhabitants.

The top predators in the pools are water beetles, dragonfly larvae and frogs, although other predators stake out bromeliad tanks in order to catch a meal. The slant-faced katydid, a relative of the grasshopper, wades into the tank to catch insects. Vine snakes and long-legged crane hawks catch visiting frogs. In fact, while the bromeliad pool is like an aquarium tank, the surrounding area is similar to a 'terrarium' with its own community of preying mantises, scorpions, spiders, snakes and lizards.

HIGH-RISE CONFLICT A freshwater crab threatens to take over the bromeliad pool in which a strawberry poison-dart frog has deposited a tadpole.

Frog nurseries and refuges

Most frogs use a bromeliad tank to deposit their eggs and rear their tadpoles, and sometimes the demand can be so high parents come to blows. Male poison-dart frogs wrestle for the right to occupy tanks because they attract females. Depending on the species, either male or female frogs carry eggs or tadpoles on their back and deposit them in a tank, where they complete their development into froglets.

The female strawberry poison-dart frog of South and Central America lays just three to five eggs in a jelly-like mass on a leaf. The male visits them often, using water from its cloaca to keep them moist. When the eggs hatch, the female carries the tadpoles on her back up to the canopy where, because they are likely to eat one another, they are placed in separate bromeliad pools. Having established all the offspring in vacant pools the frog returns to them every two to three days, depositing a couple of unfertilised eggs in each pool on which the tadpoles can feed.

One species of frog has adopted the bromeliad tank as a refuge. During the day, it sits in the centre of the leaf whorl and hunkers down in a unique way. The top of its head is flattened with a bony lid that fits snugly into the bromeliad's central tube and its eyes sink into its mouth cavity. Hidden like this, it is safe from predators and from drying out. The bromeliad also profits from this visitor – the living 'plug' prevents water in the tank from evaporating.

Crabs in the treetops

In the remnant tropical rain forests of Jamaica, bromeliad pools host unexpected youngsters – baby crabs. The adults are freshwater crabs, less than 2.5 cm long and flattened so that they can squeeze between the leaves of bromeliads. They spend their entire lives in the trees, and the mothers are probably the most attentive mothers of any crab species. The eggs – between 20 and 200 in a brood – are deposited in the tank where they develop into tiny crab larvae.

Having deposited the eggs the mother leaves nothing to chance. During the next couple of months, it monitors and maintains the water quality by removing dead plant debris, such as leaves. The crab also circulates the water to ensure there is sufficient oxygen, and drops in tiny snail shells to add calcium and reduce the acidity of the water. Unattended pools are acidic and low in calcium and oxygen, so the young crabs would die if their mother were not so diligent. The crab also protects the brood from predators, such as the aquatic larvae of dragonflies or damselflies. Bromeliad crabs are one of the few known crab species that take such painstaking care of their offspring, but the story does not end there.

Recently scientists studying the crabs have found that not all the youngsters leave the parent tree. They form social groups, much like bees and ants. There is a queen – the only female to lay eggs – and her offspring from several breeding seasons. So the young crabs benefit not just from the attention of their mother, but also their older siblings.

WATER
WORLDS

7

RAIN FORESTS, BY THEIR VERY NATURE, HAVE A SUPERABUNDANCE OF RAINWATER. While much of it evaporates in the tropical heat, there is still run-off from the leaves that reaches the ground. Tiny rivulets amalgamate into streams and they, in turn, join together to form rivers. These are the tributaries of even larger rivers and, along with torrents that crash down from mountains upstream, they create some of the world's greatest rivers – the Amazon, Orinoco, Congo and Mekong. Rivers were – and still are – the main highways into tropical rain forests. Their waters are also home to unique assemblages of plants and animals, and they have a tremendous influence on life in the forest, sometimes flooding huge areas of it. Water power, demonstrated here by South America's mighty Iguaçu Falls (left), is central to rain-forest life.

RAIN-FOREST
RIVERS

RIVERS ARE THE ARTERIES OF THE FOREST.
Complex systems of waterways criss-cross all
of the world's major tropical rain forests, each of
them draining enormous tracts of land, many thousands of
square kilometres in area. The waterways come together to form
some of the world's greatest rivers

The mightiest of them all is the Amazon, the largest river
by volume on the planet. It and its 1100 main tributaries flow
almost 6500 km across the northern part of South America,
draining an area of 6.9 million km². They carry one-fifth of the
world's running freshwater at an average speed of 5 km/h from the
Andes to the Atlantic, delivering 200 million litres of water into
the ocean every second. The lower reaches of the river are so broad
and deep that ocean-going ships can reach Iquitos in Peru, 3700 km
from the sea, yet the drop in level from here to the mouth is just
90 m. Atlantic tides are felt 725 km from the mouth. The water
temperature in the Amazon's main channels is astonishingly stable,
fluctuating no more than a degree either side of 29°C.

Crossing continents

The world's second largest river system is that of the Congo. The
river itself is only the eighth longest in the world – flowing in a
gigantic arc some 4500 km from its source in mountains on the
borders of Zambia and the Democratic Republic of Congo to its
mouth on Africa's west coast – but it drains an area of about
3.7 million km². At its widest, the main river is 16 km across. It
has 30 waterfalls and thousands of islands, at least 50 of which
are more than 16 km long. Much of the land surrounding the river
is covered with tropical rain forest.

A third great river system associated with rain forests is
the Mekong Basin, the largest river basin in South-east Asia and
tenth largest in the world by volume. Rising in the Tibetan
Plateau, the Mekong flows for some 4880 km, reaching the
South China Sea through nine estuaries in southern Vietnam and
draining an area more than twice the size of Germany. The Lower
Mekong Basin has the most productive river fishery in the world.
The river as a whole is home to between 1200 and 1700 fish
species, the highest fish diversity in any basin after the Amazon
and Congo. Sixty-two species are found nowhere else in the
world, including the Laotian shad (a freshwater herring), which
travels thousands of kilometres upriver to spawn. It was once
the most abundant fish in the river, but overfishing, dams and
pollution have had a serious impact on its numbers.

MUDDY WATERS The coffee colour of the Amazon is
caused by silt washed down from the young rocks of the
Andes. Some tributaries are like dark tea, the result of
tannins washed from leaves. Others are clear blue-green,
having run over older rocks that have already eroded.

FOREST WATERWAYS
Rain-forest rivers are among the largest and longest in the world, the result of high rainfall and a large catchment area.

RIVER	LENGTH (km)	DRAINAGE AREA (km²)	AVERAGE DISCHARGE PER SECOND (m³)	FLOWS INTO
Amazon (South America)	6296	6 915 000	219 000	Atlantic Ocean
Congo (Africa)	4371	3 680 000	41 800	Atlantic Ocean
Mekong (Asia)	4023	810 000	16 000	South China Sea
Purús (South America)	3379	63 166	8 400	Amazon River
Madeira (South America)	3238	850 000	17 000	Amazon River
Japurá (South America)	2615	242 259	6 000	Amazon River
Juruá (South America)	2410	200 000	6 000	Amazon River
Ubangi (Africa)	2300	unknown	unknown	Congo River
Orinoco (South America)	2101	880 000	31 900	Caribbean Sea
Sepik (Asia)	1126	77 700	unknown	Bismarck Sea

DOLPHINS IN THE TREETOPS, PIRANHAS EATING NUTS AND SLOTHS SWIMMING – this is not a world turned upside down, but a description of everyday events in the Amazon when the river breaks its banks and the adjacent rain forest is flooded.

From December to May each year, the ice and snow in the Andes thaw, and the resulting meltwater rushes down into the Amazon Basin. Combined with the effects of torrential rainfall during the wet season from January to April, this raises the water level in the channels of the main river and its major tributaries by 9–14 m.

For around 7.5 km on either side of the river, the water backs up and inundates the forest, creating a vast slow-moving, tree-filled lake – the Amazon's flooded forest. Beside 'white' water rivers that flow directly from the Andes, the flooded forest is known as the *varzia*. Beside 'black' water rivers, which are coloured with tannins from decaying leaves, it is called the *igapo*. All in all, the flooded forest covers an area of more than 250 000 km².

Escaping the waters

When rivers overflow like this, animals have to change their habits. Creatures that normally live on the ground take to the trees. Somehow, many seem to know that the water is rising and start climbing even before it reaches them. Some insects that fail to

Creatures that normally live on the ground take to the trees. Somehow, many seem to know that the water is rising and start climbing even before it reaches them.

FLOODED FOREST

reach dry zones can float to safety, relying on the surface tension of the water to keep them on top. Fire-ant colonies form into living balls and drift to the nearest land or tree. Predators have a field day. Preying mantises and spiders stake out the rain-forest trees and intercept any insects coming up from the ground. Needlefish wait below and grab anything that falls out of the trees.

Even people and their domestic stock must adapt to the flood. The local river people, called *ribeirinhos*, have houses on stilts or homes that float. Chickens and even cattle are corralled for the next few months on separate rafts.

Fish and nuts

This is the period when many forest trees set seed, and for a number of these trees it is fish that distribute their seeds. Silver dollars or pacus, matrinchás and several types of catfish eat the fleshy parts of smaller fruits, the seeds passing through their gut unharmed. Some species of piranha crack the nuts hidden inside larger fruits. These fish include the metre-long tambaqui, a seed-predator whose nasal flap actually detects the biochemical changes taking place in trees that are about to fruit. It can then hang

RIVER JUNCTION The silt-filled waters of the Amazon's upper reaches meet the black waters of its tributary, the Rio Negro. They do not mix for many kilometres downstream. Seen from the air, there is a distinct boundary between the water from the two rivers.

about in the right place, attracted to the fruits as they plop into the water and smashing them open with nut-cracking jaws.

High water is the best time for fish to breed, because the greater volume of water means that they are less likely to be spotted by predators. Despite that, many fish take no chances, and parental care is common among Amazonian fishes. The fry of the aruaña hide inside their parent's mouth. The tamoatá surrounds its eggs with a raft of bubbles, which serves a double purpose. It provides the fish's offspring with enough oxygen and also resembles frogspawn, so predators think twice about eating it. The loricaria fish glues eggs to its body, while the fry of the discus fish graze

mucous on their parents' bodies. Cichlids, such as the acar-boari, herd their young through 'floating meadows', rafts of vegetation that break away from the land when the forest floods.

These can be huge, more than a kilometre across, and they are crowded with wildlife. On top of a floating meadow, horned screamers – distantly related to ducks, geese and swans – graze on young water hyacinths, while jacanas with broad spindly feet catch insects. Below the raft, fish and dragonfly larvae grab small aquatic organisms. Swamp eels squirm through the vegetation, and knife fish find their way about using pulsing electric fields which they generate inside their bodies.

FLOODED FOREST DISGUISE The aptly named leaf fish resembles a leaf that has dropped into the river. It inhabits slow-moving, muddy rivers and hangs motionless in the water to catch even smaller fish.

Fish for every niche

Some of the Amazon fish are extremely small, like the neon tetras, commonly kept by aquarists, which live in the black water rivers. Some fish do not even live in the river. The trichomycterid catfish resembles a tiny red worm and makes its home in the film of water adhering to leaf litter. There are also leaf fish, which live in the river but resemble dead leaves; jaraqui, which suck up detritus; angelfish, discus fish and banded headstanders, which eat algae; and the deep-bodied hatchetfish, which can leap clear of the water and 'fly' a short distance to escape other predatory fish. The splashing tetra leaps to deposit its eggs on a leaf, and the eel-like aruaña leaps to grab insects and spiders from low branches. The candiru is a minute fish that lives as a parasite in the gills of larger fish. It also has the unfortunate habit of swimming up the urethra of anyone urinating in the water.

The most notorious of the Amazon's fishes is the red-bellied piranha, schools of which can strip a capybara – the world's largest rodent, the size of a Labrador dog (see page 100) – to a skeleton in less than two minutes. Small schools of piranha wait beneath egret nests for clumsy chicks to drop out.

The huge quantities of decaying leaves that drop into the water from rain-forest trees can sometimes starve the fish of oxygen. In relatively still conditions, the microorganisms, such as bacteria, that break down the leaves use up all the oxygen dissolved in the water as part of the process of decay. As a result, there is none left for the fish. Conditions can get so bad that hundreds of thousands of fish are sometimes found floating dead on the surface.

Some species have adaptations that enable them to survive these low oxygen levels. The tambaqui is one – it changes the

MINERALS FROM TEARS A flock of colourful butterflies harass a yellow-spotted river turtle. They are after the minerals contained in the tears at the corners of the turtle's eyes.

DEADLY ADVERSARIES A spectacled caiman gets the better of a piranha. Marauding shoals of piranhas get their own back by eating baby caimans.

shape of its lips so it can swim just below the water surface and skim off the oxygen-rich surface film. The giant 3 m long pirarucu, one of the world's largest freshwater fish, has gills like other fish when it is young, but these wither away and become less important as the pirarucu matures and turns into an air-breather. It develops a special lining to its throat that works like a lung, so the fish has to take a gulp of air every 10 to 15 minutes in order to breathe. The pirarucu is also an especially effective predator – it has teeth on its tongue that function as an extra set of jaws.

Oxbow lakes

By May, the waters are receding and the natural course of the river begins to appear once more. With such a gentle descent from thousands of kilometres inland to the estuary, the Amazon not only meanders but can also change its course, and occasionally a bend is cut off from the main channel to form an oxbow lake. The still waters provide ideal conditions for the giant water lily, a magnificent plant with the biggest floating leaves imaginable – up to 1.8 m across and able to support a small person.

As the dry season approaches and the water level drops still further, the river channels become narrower and the oxbow lakes begin to dry out. With gradually less water, fish become more concentrated and fish predators take full advantage of this time

of plenty. Neotropical cormorants flock in and drop down onto the water, arriving in such large numbers that they blacken the sky. They hunt cooperatively, forming large rafts and swimming round in ever-decreasing circles. In this way, they herd the fish into tight balls before they dive and pick them off one by one.

Also feasting on the fish bounty are giant otters, surfacing above the water with loud, horse-like blows, then disappearing again with a splash. These giant otters are as long as human beings are tall, with small ears, large eyes and webbed feet: all adaptations for hunting underwater. The whiskers on their snouts are thought to help them to detect prey. They can also close their ears and nostrils while they are below the surface.

Giant otter families often hunt together during the day, but any fish an individual takes it eats alone. Piranhas are a favourite catch, but otters also eat catfish, perch, freshwater crabs, small caiman and snakes. Elsewhere in the world, most otter species live solitary lives, but the Amazonian rivers and oxbow lakes frequented by giant otters are filled with so many fish that they can live in groups, an effective deterrent against predators, such as jaguars, large caiman and anacondas. Giant otters also help their local wildlife community – freshwater dolphins often follow them and wait for them to flush out fish into deeper water.

There are two kinds of dolphin in the Amazon: the larger boto or Amazon river dolphin and the smaller tucuxi. The boto is beautifully adapted to the murky conditions in rivers. It 'sees' with sound, using echolocation to find its way and locate fish.

The smaller spectacled caimans have a different technique. They occupy oxbow lakes where the rapidly dropping water level concentrates the fish, immersing the caimans in a living bouillabaisse. Leaping clear of the water, the caimans crash down sideways onto the trapped fish. The fish are so densely packed that a caiman can be sure of catching one every time.

The caimans themselves are harassed by an assortment of biting insects, the most persistent being tabanid horseflies. These attack the soft tissues around the caimans' eyes and nostrils and are clearly a major irritant. The caimans submerge to rid themselves of the flies, but the insects simply fly around over the water surface, waiting for the caimans to resurface. Then they renew their attacks. Less annoying are the butterflies that settle on the caiman's head to drink the salt-rich tears in the corners of its eyes. The butterflies seek out freshwater turtles for the same reason.

Turtles live in the main river channels and their breeding season begins as soon as the water drops from May onwards and sand banks are exposed. The females haul out of the water some time before they dig their nests and bask in the Sun, the warmth hastening the development of their still unlaid eggs. They need a good head start, for once laid the eggs must hatch and the baby turtles be ready to swim before the floodwaters rise once more in December. Nest space is at a premium on the sandbanks, so inevitably females dig up the eggs of turtles that nested earlier. Black vultures drop in to eat any eggs that are exposed.

By the time the waters have fully receded in August, most trees in the flooded forest have completed fruiting, but a few wait for low water. The munguba tree is one. Its bright red pods are torn apart by little star parakeets, and any debris dropping below is not wasted. South American 'river trout' or matrinchão wait below the tree and sometimes leap clear of the water in order to catch the seeds before they reach the surface.

EGG LEAP The female splashing tetra of the lower Amazon leaps clear of the water to deposit her eggs on the underside of leaves hanging over the river. The male splashes them every 10–15 minutes to stop them drying out. The fry drop into the river after a couple of days.

Although this echolocation system is relatively primitive compared with those of ocean-living dolphins, the wide beam of high-pitched sounds that emanate from the boto's forehead is perfect for navigating the treetops of the flooded forest. The boto also has a flexible neck so it can direct the sonar beam without having to move its entire body, a useful adaptation in narrow river channels where it is tight to manoeuvre.

The tucuxi has a more conventional dolphin shape, resembling the sea-going Atlantic white-sided dolphin, to which it is more closely related. It behaves just like other dolphins – hunting in small groups of 15 or more individuals, leaping, spy-hopping and tail-splashing.

Crocodile tears

The Amazon's largest crocodile species, the 4 m long black caiman, has adopted its own novel way to catch fish. Black caimans move slowly sideways, undulating their tails as they go, and they gradually drive the fish into the shallows closer to shore. They then turn rapidly and plunge with mouths agape into the boiling mass of fish.

THE GIANT WATER LILY HAS FOOTBALL-SIZED FLOWERS that are pollinated by scarab beetles. As a flower heats up, it produces a butterscotch odour attractive to the beetles. These are enticed inside the flower, where they become trapped for a short while. They are dusted with pollen, and then the flower releases them.

THE ELECTRIC EEL of the Amazon generates an electric shock of 500 volts and 1 ampere of current, a discharge dangerous to humans.

THE VAMPIRE FISH SWIMS INTO THE GILLS OF LARGER fish and sucks their blood. It is 25 mm long and transparent.

FACTS

GIANT OTTER

THE WORLD'S LARGEST OTTER SPECIES, THE GIANT OTTER OR 'RIVER WOLF' OF SOUTH AMERICA CAN BE UP TO 1.8 M LONG, ALMOST TWICE THE SIZE OF THE EUROPEAN RIVER OTTER. Its chocolate brown coat consists of dense, water-repellent fur and a velvety underfur. At its throat, it has a white or pale yellow patch, the pattern of which is different in each otter. A breeding pair lives together with an extended family of youngsters from previous years. Older siblings baby-sit the new generation, and they take it in turns so none of the family goes hungry. Youngsters are taught to swim at about two months, but some are reluctant swimmers, and the mother has to grab them and dump them in the water. They can be independent after two to three years but more often remain with the family until it becomes too large and has to split. Groups, called 'romps' or 'bevies', are generally less than a dozen strong, although some contain up to 20 otters.

VITAL STATISTICS

CLASS: Mammalia
ORDER: Carnivora
SPECIES: *Pteroneura brasiliensis*
HABITAT: Rivers and flooded forest
DISTRIBUTION: South America, except for Chile, Argentina and Uruguay
KEY FEATURE: Unusually large otter with creamy marking on its chest.

SEA IN A RIVER

BARBED TAIL A freshwater stingray rests on the bed of the Rio Negro, a tributary of the Amazon. On the top of the tail, close to the tip, is a venomous barb, which is used in defence.

Ganges, Indus and Mekong each have their own dolphin species, although all these are now extremely rare. In South America, the boto (see page 143) lives in both the Amazon and Orinoco river systems. It is the largest of the river dolphins, with a pink skin, rather than the more usual grey of ocean-going dolphins. South America's other freshwater dolphin, the tucuxi, also lives in the Amazon. Tucuxis sometimes feed alongside botos, but they need to eat twice as much as their cousins because they are so active, often trapping fish against the water surface and swimming upside down to catch them.

River sharks and freshwater rays

The Amazon, Congo and several other large rivers are visited by the 3.5 m long bull shark – a man-eater that ranks among the top ten sharks most dangerous to humans. The females enter large rivers from the sea to give birth. Sharks at sea have enemies – usually other sharks – but few others enter freshwater, so bull-shark youngsters are relatively safe in rivers. Bull sharks have been spotted as far as 4200 km from the mouth of the Amazon. Their water regulation system can cope with the transition from saltwater to freshwater, something few fish can do.

A few sharks have adapted specifically to freshwater living and inhabit the rivers of southern Asia and Queensland, Australia. They are not at all dangerous and extremely secretive. One, the 2 m long Borneo river shark, was thought to be extinct until it was rediscovered in 1998. All are fish-eaters. Because of the very limited visibility in cloudy estuarine and river waters, they rely on other senses – hearing, smell and electro-reception – rather than vision.

Skates and rays have also adapted to freshwater. Many rain-forest rivers, including the Amazon, Congo and Mekong, have freshwater stingrays. Their ancestors were marine species, which became cut off from the sea. In the Amazon, it is thought, the rays were concentrated about 100 million years ago in a shallow sea at the western end of the Amazon. Later, as the Andes began to form, the rays became isolated from the Pacific. By about 65 million years ago, the waters of their inland sea had been freshened by meltwaters from the rapidly rising mountains, and any surviving rays would have been ones able to live in freshwater.

In the Mekong, Fly and other large southern Asian and northern Australian rivers, rays grow to tremendous sizes. In 2004, a specimen caught in the Mekong River measured 2.4 m across and 5 m in length, including its tail, and weighed 600 kg. It had the largest barb (venomous spine at the end of the tail) of any known stingray – about 38 cm long. These giant fish are not common, but anglers have reeled in rays the size of dinner tables; the world record for a freshwater ray landed by rod-and-line is about 90 kg. It was caught and released again in the Bang Pakong River, Thailand.

THE ESTUARIES OF THE MAJOR RAIN-FOREST RIVERS ARE SO WIDE THAT STANDING ON ONE BANK, IT IS IMPOSSIBLE TO SEE THE OTHER. The expanse of water looks like a sea, and the resemblance is all the more striking if you dive below and see what is living in the silt-filled depths. There are all the freshwater creatures you would expect, catfish, eels and freshwater crabs, but there are also some surprises – creatures you would more expect to see in the ocean. These include the freshwater dolphins that live in the major rain-forest rivers of South America and southern Asia. In Asia, the

FRESHWATER GIANTS

JUST AS THE RAIN FORESTS ARE PACKED WITH FOOD FOR TERRESTRIAL ANIMALS, rain-forest rivers have enough food and plenty of space to support gigantic water-living creatures, the largest of their kind in the world. The Mekong, for example, not only has a giant stingray (see page 147), but also a giant catfish. The largest known specimen, caught in June 2005 in northern Thailand, was 2.7 m long and weighed 293 kg, the largest freshwater fish ever taken. In the past, hundreds of these huge fish were harvested each year, but now only a few are caught, partly because of overfishing, partly because dams have interrupted their migration route from feeding grounds in the lower river to spawning sites upstream. The giant catfish is now considered the most endangered freshwater fish on Earth.

Giant crocs and mythical snakes

The Orinoco River in north-western South America is home to the Orinoco crocodile – at 5 m long, the continent's biggest crocodile and its largest predator. Several have been known to attack and eat people, but they more usually feed on fish and other vertebrates, including birds that get too close to water. Orinoco crocodiles have long, slightly upturned snouts, and come in three distinct colours: dark grey (the negro crocodile), greyish-green with dark patches on the back (the mariposa) and light tan with dark patches (the amarillo). The amarillo is the most common.

The estuarine or saltwater crocodile of southern Asia and northern Australia is not only the world's largest living crocodile, but also its largest reptile – the longest recorded 'salty', shot in Australia, measured 8.6 m from snout to tail. Saltwater crocodiles move into swamp forests in the wet season, then relocate to estuaries in the dry. The largest males will take anything from water buffalo to large sharks. They are ambush predators that wait close to a riverbank, either submerged or so motionless that they resemble logs. When prey is within range, a salty explodes into life, accelerating through the water at up to 32 km/h. It grabs the victim and drags it into the water to drown. The crocodile then grabs the body and twists – the 'death roll' – in order to tear off manageable chunks. Sometimes the victims are people. It is estimated that more than 300 people a year are killed and eaten by saltwater crocodiles.

The anaconda, the world's heaviest snake, lives in the Amazon and Orinoco Basins. This powerful predator supports its body by lying most of the time in water. It kills its prey, such as tapirs, deer, capybara and caiman, by enveloping them in constricting coils and asphyxiating them. It then swallows them whole. Wild claims have been made for the length reached by anacondas. One of the more believable reports came from the Australian-born Vincent Roth who shot a 10.3 m specimen while working in Guyana in the mid-20th century. The US Wildlife Conservation Society offers a reward for any anaconda over 9 m delivered alive. The prize, which currently stands at US $50 000, has remained unclaimed since the early 20th century. In a recent survey in Brazil, the longest anaconda found was just 5 m.

GIANT SNAKE The yellow anaconda is one of four species of anaconda in South America. Adults average 5 m long – larger specimens have been claimed but not proven.

MONSTER FISH Local fishermen regard the Mekong catfish as sacred, for it 'meditates' in deep pools, but they still eat it. The liver is a delicacy and the female's roe is pickled as 'Laotian caviar'.

*TINY CALLERS This dainty tree
frog from Queensland, Australia,
lives in vegetation close to rivers.
The males call out for mates
after heavy rain, and sometimes
synchronise their calling so the
sound travels further.*

FOREST FROGS

THE GOLDEN TOAD WAS A TINY CREATURE, BARELY 5 CM
LONG, WHICH LIVED IN HIGH-ALTITUDE FORESTS IN COSTA
RICA. The male's body was bright orange and its skin
shiny, unlike the skin of many other toads; the female
was a dull olive colour with scarlet spots. The toads lived mostly
underground, but in the breeding season males gathered in breeding
sites around puddles, waiting for females. One biologist described
the males as resembling 'dazzling jewels on the forest floor'.

Scientists first discovered the golden toad in 1966, and it
quickly became iconic, featuring on posters that celebrated the
biodiversity of Costa Rica's rain forests. Just 23 years later, they were
all gone. In 2004, the International Union for the Conservation of
Nature and Natural Resources declared the species extinct.

Frogs of all kinds

Rain-forest frog and toad populations are large and varied. More than 80 species
were recently discovered in a 3 km² plot in Ecuador, and new species are being
discovered all the time. They range in size from the world's largest frog – the
goliath frog of the Congo – to some of the smallest, such as the poison-dart frogs
of South America. There are glass frogs, so transparent that their bones and
internal organs show through their skins, and gastric breeding frogs, which have

tadpoles developing inside their stomachs. Other frogs wave brightly coloured feet, rather than croak, because their voices would be drowned out by the waterfalls they sit beside.

Frog populations are a good way to gauge the health of a rain forest. They are what scientists call 'indicator' species – plants or animals highly sensitive to changes in their environment. Frogs like moist habitats, and rain-forest species are only comfortable when living in at least 80 per cent humidity. They take in chemicals through the skin, as well as through the lining of the mouth and throat, so any pollution in the environment will find its way into their bodies. Frogs are also found at all levels in the forest. Anything that happens to them will affect the entire ecosystem.

Currently, rain-forests frogs are telling us that something is wrong. Since 1989, 20 out of 40 species have disappeared from a 30 km^2 study area in the Monteverde Cloud Forest of Costa Rica. Habitat destruction is one likely reason for this loss, as is climate change. Frogs tend to live in precise niches in the habitat, so tiny changes in temperature and humidity can affect them. Disease is another factor, also linked with climate change. Scientists studying the Central American harlequin frog have shown that higher global temperatures result in more clouds over tropical forests, especially in upland areas, producing cooler days and warmer nights – the right conditions for the disease-bearing chytrid fungus to flourish. All this adds up to a crisis for rain-forest frog populations. It is estimated that a third of the world's frog species are likely to disappear, the first major catastrophe linked to global warming.

TOXIC FROG Unlike many other frogs, the blue poison-dart frog lacks webbing between the toes and is a poor swimmer. South American Indians use toxins from its skin on the tips of their blowgun darts.

FUTURE OF
RAIN FORESTS

AT ONE TIME, RAIN FORESTS WERE ALMOST IMPENETRABLE. Lumberjacks had to journey in by river; they cut down trees by hand and logs were floated down to the coast along the same rivers. Today, all that has changed. Roads and railways, industrial chainsaws, huge caterpillar tractors and flatbed trucks have opened up the forests and made logging easier and quicker. The result is the loss of 70 000–170 000 km²

of tropical rain forest worldwide each year. Five generations ago, great swathes of rain forest covered the world's land surface. Today, apart from the Amazon and Congo, two-thirds of the surviving forests exist just as patchy remnants. Higher levels of carbon dioxide in the atmosphere and the consequent global warming mean that rain-forest trees are growing faster and bigger than they used to (see page 31), but that does not help. If there are no forests left, there are no trees to grow in the first place.

The importance of the rain-forest habitat goes far beyond the forest itself. They are important in storing carbon, maintaining the balance of gases in the atmosphere, producing oxygen and regulating global weather systems. They are unparalleled in biological diversity and as a natural reservoir for genetic diversity. Millions of species of plants and animals live there, many of which could be of value as foods or medicines.

All this makes the loss of rain forests a tragedy not just for the species and communities that live in them. In many ways, they are still mysterious places, which hold countless secrets, including plants and animals yet to be discovered. With the forests disappearing so fast, the danger is that those secrets – many of which could be beneficial to humans – will go with them.

Demand high

Logging is the most obvious threat to the rain forests. Tropical forest trees have evolved to resist attacks from fungi, bacteria and insects, so they are ideal for the manufacture of garden furniture, decking and any other product that has to stand outside in the worst of the weather. The timber, which includes teak and mahogany, is called 'tropical hardwood', and it is in great demand. Nowadays, a single log of teak can command a price of around US $20 000.

Until now, the largest single source of tropical hardwoods has been South-east Asia, but the forests there are disappearing fast due not only to the activities of legitimate logging companies, but also to illegal logging operations. In places such as Indonesia, where islands are widely spread out and policing is difficult, it is thought that 70 per cent of the logging is illegal. If the current rate of deforestation continues, it is estimated that primary rain forests in the region will disappear in the next five years.

African forests, such as those of Côte d'Ivoire and Nigeria, have already been decimated. Attention now focuses on the tropical forests of South and Central America. Clearing the forests for ranching, sugar-cane production for biofuel, charcoal for smelting and subsistence farming has already had an impact. New threats come not just from commercial logging. Extensive reserves of oil, gas, gold, iron, bauxite and other minerals lie beneath the ground. If the present rate of tropical deforestation continues, nearly all the primary rain forest in the Amazon will have gone within the next 50 years.

CITY FORESTS Tijuca National Park is one of the world's largest urban forests. It is part of Brazil's Atlantic coast rain forest – an isolated patch in the city of Rio de Janeiro.

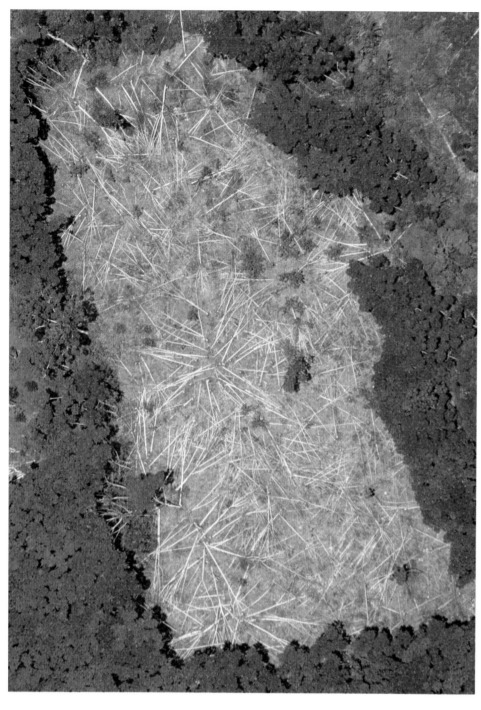

FOREST GOING, GOING, GONE An aerial photograph shows a patch of Amazon forest that has been clear-felled prior to burning. The nutrients will go up in smoke, leaving a sterile landscape unfit for long-term farming.

In 2007, the western lowland gorilla was added to the 'critically endangered' category of the World Conservation Union's Red List, even though there are still tens of thousands of the animals living in the wild. The measure was taken because of the risk that Ebola could wipe them all out in a single outbreak. In this case, there is an answer to the problem, and a simple one. Sharpshooters seek out the gorillas and shoot them – not with bullets, but with darts containing a vaccine against Ebola. Vaccines have become a conservation tool.

What's to be done?

When it comes to rain-forest destruction as a whole, scientists and politicians now realise that no simple solution exists. Measures such as banning the international trade in rain-forest timbers or establishing nature reserves where no humans are allowed to go are unlikely to work. Even if the necessary reserves are set up right away, the estimate is that only 5 per cent of species will be protected and survive.

One suggestion is to establish multi-purpose reserves, which promote sustainable development from the moment they are set up – people and nature working in harmony. This would take account not only of the needs of plants and animals, but also of the humans living there. After all, forest peoples such as the Congo pygmies, the Semang and Penan of Malaysia and the Yanomami of the Amazon have been living in the rain forest for thousands of years without harming it.

Another suggestion is to replant areas of forest that have been cleared, but there is a fundamental problem with this. All the nutrients in a tropical rain forest are locked up in the trees. Remove the trees wholesale over large areas and most of the nutrients go with them. Any nutrients remaining are lost as heavy rainfall erodes the land and leaches out essential minerals. The entire area is turned into a wasteland, no longer viable for growing trees and virtually useless as agricultural land except in the very short term. Yet some countries, especially those in the Amazonian forest, have encouraged their poor to eke out a living by clearing rain forest. In 1995, a NASA satellite survey recorded nearly 40 000 individual fires related to forest clearance in Brazil. This was four times the number seen in the same month the previous year, and the destruction increases year on year.

Rain-forest legacy

It is estimated that upwards of 20 000 species may be going extinct every year. With some species, this happens before they have been described or named, which means one species could be dying out every half-hour and we do not even know it.

To make matters worse, many rain-forest species are threatened by more than habitat destruction. The gorillas and other higher apes of Central Africa, for example, live – literally – in a war zone due to political instability in the region. They are also a target for the bush-meat trade and, even more disturbingly, they are susceptible to diseases that affect humans, including the devastating Ebola virus. This killer can be passed from gorillas to humans and vice versa.

Company policy

A number of large international companies that rely on timber for their products, such as IKEA and Home Depot, are taking steps to try to improve matters. Working with a coalition of groups called Global Forest Watch – an initiative of the World Resources Institute, a Washington-based environmental think-tank – they discourage irresponsible and illegal logging by committing themselves to 'responsibly harvested' timber.

Another approach is the concept of 'ecosystem services', adopted by the Natural Capital Project of Stanford University in California, the Nature Conservancy and WWF. This puts a monetary value on the services that the healthy rain forest provides, including prevention of soil erosion and regulating oxygen and carbon dioxide levels. The theory is that a financial incentive is more effective than, say, a moral duty or relying on the beauty of a resource to attract conservationists' attention. Tourism statistics and land use information can be employed to establish ecotourism revenue, which shows, for instance, how logging would reduce the real value of a forest. The danger is that if a species or ecosystem is unlikely to pay its way, it will be ignored or even sacrificed in favour of a more valuable entity.

More and more, it is becoming clear to experts that the key to the rain forests' future is understanding not only their biology and geology, but also their social complexities. Since 1950, the world's population has doubled, with the fastest growth occurring

FACTS

MORE THAN 2000 TROPICAL RAIN-FOREST PLANTS ARE known to have anti-cancer properties. Over 100 US pharmaceutical companies and government agencies now have research programmes searching for medicines in the world's rain forests.

EVERY SECOND an area of rain forest the size of a football field is being cut down. That is about 31 million football fields per year.

ONLY 6 PER CENT OF TROPICAL RAIN FORESTS are protected worldwide.

FACTS

in the tropics, so that today there are more people living in the tropics than the total world population in 1950. This growing population needs space and food. If the correct decisions are not made soon, the reverberations will be felt not only in the rain forests themselves, but right across the entire planet.

NEW FORESTS On a sustainable development reserve in Brazil, timber is harvested and trees replanted. There are problems even with these reserves. Ultimately, a rain forest is more valuable alive, as a source of medicines, fruits, nuts and oils, than dead as timber.

INDEX

A

acids 132, 135
Africa 16, 17, 21, 23, 37, 41, 46, 58, 65, 67, 69, 73, 75, 80, 84, 86, 87, 89, 91, 95, 98, 99, 100, 101, 102, 104, 110, 111, 113–114, 116, 117, 119, 121, 128, 153, 154
agoutis 46, 114, 133
Alaska 38, 40
alerces 40
algae 34, 51, 134, 142
aluminium oxide 32
Amazon River 26–27, 32, 133, 137, 138–139, 140–141, 143, 144, 147
    Amazon Basin 16, 26, 27, 32, 139, 140, 149
Amazonia 17, 29, 31, 35, 36, 46, 50, 53, 54, 58, 63, 65, 72, 76, 77, 100, 102, 106, 110, 114, 116, 119, 121, 127, 153, 154
    Peruvian Amazon 104, 131
Ambon (Indonesia) 37
amino acids 30, 31
ammonia 133
amphibians 6, 20, 65
anacondas 112, 115, 143, 148–149
Ancistrocladus korupensis 37
Andes 17, 27, 32, 37, 40, 114, 139, 140, 147
angelfish 142
animals 62–81
    co-existence of 124–135
    food for 82–107
    larger animals 100–101, 106–107, 148–149
    in rivers 138–151
    smaller animals 96–99, 112
anoas 25, 99
anomalures 66, 67
ant bears 119
ant plants 57
antbirds 116
anteaters 28, 65, 118, 119, 128
antelopes 71, 98, 101, 111
antibiotics 37, 71
ants 28, 71, 118, 119, 126, 127, 128
    army 106, 109, 116
    Azteca 116, 131
    Barteria 131
    Crematogaster 127
    driver 109, 116–117, 128
    fire 140
    green 127
    leafcutter 4, 126, 128
    predatory 116–117
    schmitzi 132
    'white ants' (termites) 128
antshrikes 116
apes 68–71, 94, 154
Appalachian Mountains 40

araroba trees 37
Argentina 40
aruaña 141, 142
Asia 17, 20, 24, 46, 80, 86, 91, 99, 112, 113, 119, 147, 149
    see also South-east Asia
Aspilia species 37, 71
Atiu swiftlets 20
Atlantic Ocean 27, 41, 139
Australasia 24, 65, 93, 112, 122
Australia 20, 29, 41, 45, 53, 54, 56–57, 64, 67, 74, 77, 80, 81, 84, 85, 91, 92, 93, 103, 114, 147, 149, 150
aye-ayes 21, 23

B

babirusas 25
baboons 86
bacteria 34, 44, 102, 103, 126, 128, 132, 133, 142, 153
Bali 24
bananas 3, 36
bandicoots 46, 113
Bang Pakong River 147
Bangladesh 114
bark 33, 127
bark-eaters 87, 94
Barteria trees 131
Batanta Island 79
bats 6, 21, 57, 58, 59, 61, 74, 85, 94, 105, 106, 107, 114
    free-tail 61
    fruit 44, 92, 93, 126
    fruit-eating 85
    long-tongued 6
    nectar-feeding 49, 85
    tent-making 3, 48
    vampire 105, 122–123
    wrinkle-lipped 61
beans, Calabar 37
bears, sun 96, 97, 98
beeches 40, 41
bees 49, 50, 119, 126, 130
    orchid 57, 133
    stingless 128
    sweat 34, 129
    trigonid 126, 127
beetles 34, 35, 46, 107, 116
    dung 34, 35
    rhinoceros 107
    scarab 144
    trilobite 106
    water 134
Belize 16, 28
berries 38, 41, 91, 92, 93, 96
Bili-Bondo region (Congo) 69
binturongs 65
birches 41
biodiversity 12, 39, 63, 153
birds 6, 12, 20, 22, 25, 49, 50, 57, 59, 61, 74, 81, 87, 91–92, 96, 105, 106, 111, 113, 114, 115, 120, 121, 122, 128, 132
    see also individual species
bird's-nest soup 60, 61

birds of paradise 77, 78–79, 92
Bismarck Sea 139
Black Sea 41
bladderwort 134
blood-feeders 122–123, 144
blowgun darts 151
Blue Mountains (Oregon) 40
boas 61, 81, 105, 127
Bolivia 16, 18
bonobos 20, 68, 70–71
boongaries 103
Borneo 17, 24, 37, 52–53, 54, 57, 60, 61, 65, 81, 86–87, 94, 96, 102, 106, 107, 113, 132, 147
boron 31
boto dolphins 143, 144, 147
bowerbirds 49–50, 79, 92
Brazil 16, 18, 27, 29, 31, 37, 65, 115, 149, 152–153, 154, 155
Brazil nut tree 133
breadnut trees 89
Britain 41
bromeliads 12, 33, 56, 65, 125, 134–135
bryophytes 41
buffaloes 25, 149
bugs 35, 123, 131
Buru (Indonesia) 25
bush babies 21, 25, 69
bushmeat 71, 154
butterflies 12, 20, 34, 49, 53, 58, 59, 63, 74, 85, 93, 142, 144
    ant 116
    birdwing 53, 85
    crackers 93
    Euphaedra 93
    evening brown 93
    heliconid 53
    marsh fritillary 41
    morpho 44, 53, 58, 59, 85, 93
    owl 73, 93
    skipper 34
Butung 99

C

caimans 34, 115, 149
    black 144
    spectacled 105, 143, 144
calabash species 50
calcium 31, 32, 34, 104, 135
California 38–39
calls, animal 46, 70, 72–74, 75
Cambodia 18, 101, 113
Cameroon 17, 18, 37, 75, 92, 96
camouflage 46, 51, 53, 80–81, 101, 114
Canada 41
cancer 36, 37, 155
candirus 142
cannonball trees 50
canopy *see under* forests
capybaras 100–100, 115, 142, 149
carbohydrates 94, 131
carbon 30, 31, 153
carbon dioxide 28, 30, 31, 52, 122, 153, 155

carbon equation 30
Caribbean 17, 139
carnivores 22, 107, 113, 114, 115, 145
cassowaries 92, 104
catbirds, tooth-billed 79
caterpillars 5, 35, 45, 51, 52, 53, 131
catfish 140, 142, 143, 147
    Mekong giant 148, 149
cats 6, 12, 25, 40, 109, 112–115
cattle 32, 100, 101, 140
cave swiftlets 61
caves, rain-forest 60–61
centipedes 46, 61, 106–107
Central Africa 91, 95, 100, 101, 104, 154
Central African Republic 17
Central America 3, 5, 6, 16, 28, 44, 45, 48, 50, 51, 59, 65, 72–73, 76, 89, 103, 104, 105, 107, 110, 115, 116, 122, 135, 151, 153
chameleons 46, 65, 80, 81
chemicals 116, 119, 123, 126, 128, 151
cherries 91, 93
chevrotains, water 98
chickens 116, 140
Chile 40
Chiloé islands 40
chimpanzees 20, 68–70, 71, 89, 104
chloride 31
chlorophyll 29, 31, 48
chowchillas 46
Chronos Archipeligo 40
cicadas 49, 123
cichlids 141
Cinchona species 37
cinchona trees 36
civets 21, 25, 111
    civet-genet family 65
    civet-mongoose family 22
clay-eaters 104, 105
climate 13, 26–29
    climate change 31, 101, 151
    microclimate 27
    see also global warming
climbers (animals) 65
climbers (plants) 48
coatis 5, 111, 114
Coca River 17, 18–19
cock-of-the-rocks 77
cockatoos 91, 104
cockroaches 34, 46, 61, 116, 128
Colombia 16
colonies, animal 126–128
Congo 59, 71, 75, 86, 91, 92, 111, 118, 130, 131, 150, 153, 154
Congo, Democratic Republic of 17, 18, 139
Congo, Republic of 17
Congo River 69, 70, 137, 139, 147
    Congo Basin 17, 27, 139
Cook Islands 20
copper 31
cormorants 143

Costa Rica 6, 16, 57, 74, 83, 150, 151
Côte d'Ivoire 89, 153
cougars (pumas) 114
courtship displays (by birds) 76–79
crabs 61, 87, 134, 135, 143, 147
crickets 46, 49, 61
crocodiles 148, 149
curare vine 37
curassows 34
cuscuses 45, 64, 65, 111
cyanide 23, 102

D
Danum Valley (Sabah) 17, 58
decomposition 30, 45, 52
deer 41, 46, 61, 101, 105, 111, 112, 114, 115, 149
    lesser mouse 98, 99
Deer Cave (Sarawak) 61
deforestation 13, 32, 39, 41, 153–155
dietary supplements 104–105
dipterocarps 25, 58, 59, 111
discus fish 142
diseases 36, 37, 151, 154
DNA 30, 31
doldrums 27
dolphins 140, 143, 144, 147
Dominica 17
dragonflies 134, 141
Drakensberg mountains 41
drugs, medicinal 23, 37
    see also medicines
dry season 28–29, 58
duikers 71, 98, 99, 111
Duisburg Zoo (Germany) 22
dung 34, 35, 91, 99
durian fruit 94

E
eagles 77
    crowned 74
    crowned hawk 68
    harpy 44, 46, 59, 110
    kapul 111
    monkey-eating 73, 87, 109, 110, 111
Ebola virus 154
echidnas 119
echolocation 23, 143, 144
ecosystems 52, 61, 63, 83, 132, 134, 151
ecotourism 155
Ecuador 16, 17, 18–19, 42–43, 121, 150
eels 144, 147
eggs
    birds' 65, 96, 111
    crabs' 135
    fish 141, 142, 144
    frogs' 134, 135
    insects' 5, 116, 127, 130, 131
    turtles' 115, 144

elephants 41, 71, 91, 92, 95, 98, 104, 105
    pygmy 96
emergents 32, 33, 58, 59, 111
endangered species 22, 25, 70, 96, 99, 113, 148
enzymes 31, 35, 132, 134
epiphytes 33–34, 56–57, 83, 131, 134
Equatorial Guinea 17
estuaries 146–147, 149
Europe 38, 41, 63, 80
evaporation 134, 137
extinct species 13, 113, 150, 154
eye-spots 73, 74
eyes and eyesight 46, 54, 101

F
ferns 12, 13, 33, 38, 41, 49, 56, 83
figbird 94
figs 36, 90, 93, 94, 130, 131
    strangler 48–49
Fiji 3
fir trees 38, 40, 41
fish 6, 22, 25, 86, 87, 93, 114, 115, 139, 140, 141, 142–143, 144, 147
fish-eaters 147, 148
flies 34, 35, 122, 126
flooding 140–144
flower-eaters 3, 103
flowers 28, 33, 50, 52, 53, 57, 58, 59, 74, 84, 85, 87, 130, 131, 133
Fly River 147
'flying' animals 66–67
    flying foxes 24, 44, 92
food (for animals) 82–107
food (for humankind) 36–37
forests 42–61
    Atlantic coast forest (Brazil) 29, 31, 65, 152–153
    canopy 6, 12, 43, 44, 46, 52–57, 64, 65, 67, 73, 74, 76, 81, 87, 90, 102, 109, 111, 119, 125, 134
    Chugach National Forest 40
    Colchian forests 41
    disappearing 18, 153–155
    forest floor 5, 6, 40, 41, 43, 44, 45, 46–47, 126
    future of 152–155
    Great Bear Rain Forest 41
    Kakamega Forest 17
    Kinabalu Forest 106
    Knysna-Amatole Forest 41
    Magellanic forests 40, 41
    Monteverde Cloud Forest 151
    overstorey 43, 44, 58–59
    rain-forest recycling 30–35
    Sundarbans forests 114
    temperate forests 38–41
    threatened forests 41, 153–155
    Tongass National Forest 40
    tropical forests 3–4, 12–13, 14–37
    understorey 38, 43, 45, 48–50, 66, 74, 83, 89, 93, 122, 131

Valdivian forests 40, 41
    see also deforestation
formic acid 127
fossas 21, 22
fossils 13
fowl, Moluccan scrub 25
French Guiana 14–15, 16, 29
frogs 35, 46, 54, 81, 87, 106, 115, 128, 132, 134, 135, 150–151
    coqui 74
    gastric breeding 150
    glass 44, 150
    golden palm tree 6
    goliath 150
    harlequin 151
    harlequin flying 67
    mud-puddle 74
    poison-dart 124–125, 134, 135, 150, 151
    tree 6, 12, 150–151
    Wallace's flying 67
    White's tree 80–81
fruit 25, 34, 35, 36, 41, 44, 50, 53, 54, 65, 74, 83, 90–95, 107, 133, 155
fruit-eaters 3, 5, 29, 46, 47, 49, 52–53, 61, 70, 71, 73, 85, 86, 87, 89, 90–95, 96, 98, 99, 100, 101, 103, 104, 107, 140, 141
fry (of fish) 141, 144
fungi 29, 32, 34, 35, 40, 44, 46, 107, 126, 128, 133, 151, 153
    mycorrhizal 32, 34, 56, 133

G
Gabon 17, 75, 86, 87
Ganges River 147
geckos 49, 65, 67, 74
Georgia 41
gerygones, brown 45
gibbons 35, 72, 73, 94, 113
gliding animals 66–67
Global Forest Watch 155
global warming 17, 30, 31, 86, 153
    see also climate
gnats 132
gorillas 17, 20, 68, 69, 70, 71, 104, 154
gourd, Asian climbing 59
Great Rift Valley 17
greenhouse gases 30
guano 61
Guatemala 16
guenons 86, 87, 89
Guiana Highlands 27
Guinea 75
gums 83, 87, 89
Gunung Mulu National Park 61
Guyana 16
gymnosperms, climbing 48

H
habitat loss 98, 99, 113, 151, 154
Halmahera Island 79
hatchetfish 142

hawk-eagle, crowned 110, 111
hawks 65, 134
headstanders, banded 142
hearing 46, 95
heliconia 4, 85
hemipterans 123
herbivores 102, 112
    large 100–101
    small 96–99
hibiscus 3
hippopotamuses, pygmy 98, 99
hoatzin birds 102
hogs 100
Honduras 16, 18
honey bears 5, 65
honey mushrooms 40
honeyeaters 84, 98
Honshu island 41
hornbills 74, 91, 92, 104, 111, 127
    black-casqued 92
    Sulawesi red-knobbed 90
    white-thighed 92
    yellow-casqued 73
horseflies, tabanid 144
hummingbirds 49, 50, 84, 85
    crowned woodnymph 85
    hermit 4
    violet-fronted brilliant 84
hydrocarbons 30
hydrogen cyanide 107
hyphae 32, 34

I
Ice Age 13, 16, 17, 20
Iguaçu Falls 136–155
iguanas 3, 53, 110, 111
illness see diseases
India 21, 37, 86, 91, 93, 98, 113
Indian Ocean 21, 41, 132
Indian subcontinent 20
indicator species 151
Indonesia 18, 20, 24, 25, 29, 37, 47, 48, 79, 81, 99, 153
indris 21, 23, 72
Indus River 147
insect-eaters 29, 45, 46, 67, 87, 89, 93, 94, 99, 118–119, 127, 141, 142
insects 28, 44, 49, 50, 52, 53, 54, 57, 59, 65, 74, 106, 107, 114, 116, 121, 125, 126, 130–133, 134, 140, 144, 153
    see also individual species
Intertropical Convergence Zone (ICZ) 27
invertebrates, large 106–107
Iquitos 139
iron 31, 153
iron oxide 32

J
jaguarondis 114
jaguars 45, 46, 48, 77, 101, 105, 112, 114, 115, 143
Jamaica 135

Japan 41
Japurá River 139
jaraquis 142
Java 24, 73, 96
Juruá River 139

K

kangaroos, musky rat 91
kapok trees 58
katydids 53, 134
Kenya 17
kinkajous 5, 65
Kirishima-Yaku National Park 41
knife fish 141
kodkods 40
Komodo dragon 25
Kyushu island 41

L

lakes, oxbow 143, 144
langurs 87
Laos 101, 113
larvae 35, 116, 122, 126, 132, 134, 141
leaf-eaters 3, 29, 45, 52, 57, 87, 89, 94, 99, 102–103, 107, 131
leaf fish 141, 142
leaf-hoppers 53
leaf-insects 53
leaf litter 12, 34, 45, 46, 142
leaves 34, 52, 56, 71, 126
leeches 57, 106, 122
leks 76, 77, 79
lemurs 21, 22, 23, 73, 107
leopards 69, 71, 73, 74, 113, 114
leukaemia 23, 37
lianas 12, 33, 37, 48, 64, 131
lichens 12, 41, 46, 56
light, battle for 42–61
lizards 46, 53, 54, 65, 74, 80, 87, 96, 111, 128, 132, 134
    anole 74
    black-bearded gliding 66
    Boyd's forest dragon 93
    Draco 66, 67
    Komodo dragon 25
    monitor 111
    orange-bearded gliding 66–67
    water monitor 24, 25
log-runners 46
logging 17, 153–155
Lombok (Indonesia) 24
loricaria fish 141
lorikeets, blue-fronted 25
lorises 21, 54
lyrebirds 74

M

macaques 25, 86, 87, 113
macaws 59, 104
Madagascar 21–23, 22, 23, 29, 37, 45, 65, 72, 80, 85, 93, 107
Madeira River 139
maggots 132

magnesium 31, 32, 104
mahogany 36, 59, 153
mahogany gliders 67
malaria 23, 36
Malay Archipeligo 24, 59
Malaysia 17, 20, 39, 47, 53, 67, 101, 113, 114, 154
maleos 25
mammals 20, 22, 51, 75, 92, 106, 111, 113, 114, 115, 122, 145
    egg-laying 119
    size of 98
    see also individual species
'man-eaters' 114, 147, 149
manakins 76, 77
mandrils 75
mangabeys 89
Mangaia kingfishers 20
manganese 31, 104
mangosteen family 37
mantises (mantids) 53, 134, 140
Manu National Park 63
maples 38, 91
margays 114
Marin County 38–39
marmosets 89
marsupials 20, 40, 41, 45, 46, 64, 65, 67, 113, 114
Masoala Peninsula (Madagascar) 23
matrinchãs 140, 144
Mauritius 74
medicines 37, 104, 153, 155
    Chinese traditional 96, 98, 113
    medicinal plants 23, 36–37, 71, 155
    natural 36–37, 96
Mekong River 137, 139, 147, 148
meltwaters 140, 147
membranes, flying 66, 67
Mentawai Islands 102
methane 31
Mexico 17, 37
mice 87, 106, 107, 115
    flying 66, 67
    marsupial 113
Michelia trees 35
microclimate 27
midges 122, 132, 134
millipedes 34, 46, 106, 107, 116
mimicry 53, 74, 116
mineral reserves 153
minerals 31, 32, 34, 71, 94, 95, 105, 127, 142
mites 132
molybdenum 31
Monito del Monte 40, 65
monitors *see under* lizards
monkey puzzles 40
monkeys 6, 12, 21, 23, 35, 52, 64, 69, 73, 74, 75, 86–89, 91, 92, 105, 109, 110, 111, 114, 115, 134
    blue 87
    capuchin 50, 65, 107
    colobus 69, 89, 102, 103
    Diana 73, 89

Goelding's 89
    howler 3, 29, 35, 64, 72–73, 89, 103
    leaf 87
    mona 87
    night (or owl) 5, 54
    olive colobus 89
    proboscis 29, 102, 103, 113
    red-tailed 87
    spider 64, 89, 105
    squirrel 82–83
    Sykes 87
    uakari 52
    white-faced saki 89
    woolly 35, 89
    woolly spider 65
    see also guenons; langurs; macaques; mangabeys; marmosets; talapoins; tamarins
Montgomery State Reserve 38
mosquitoes 6, 122, 132, 134
mosses 13, 46, 56, 65
moths 29, 35, 50, 51, 53, 54, 74, 85, 105
    Atlas 54–55
    four o'clock 85
    giant Hercules 85
    hawk 5, 85
    Hercules 54
    Morgan's sphinx 85
    noctuid 93, 94
    white witch 54
    zodiac 85
Mount Adams 40
Mozambique Channel 21
mu-nam (water pig) 46
munguba trees 144

N

national parks 13, 38, 39, 41, 61, 63, 152–153
nectar-feeders 5, 6, 49, 50, 83, 84–85, 89, 93, 107, 126, 130
needlefish 140
Nepenthes genera 132
nests
    birds' 127
    insects' 127, 128
New Caledonia 65, 132
New Guinea 20, 24, 45, 46, 67, 74, 78–79, 80, 81, 92, 93, 111
New Zealand 41
Niah Cave (Sarawak) 60
Nicaragua 16
nickel 31
Nigeria 18, 153
nightlife 54–55
nitrogen 31, 49, 93, 116, 132, 134
North America 38, 40, 52, 107, 114
nut-eaters 46, 103, 140
nutrients 31, 32, 33, 40, 45, 48, 49, 56, 89, 91, 94, 103, 123, 126, 133, 154
    recycling of 34–35

nuts 44, 50, 52, 83, 90–94, 96, 99, 155
    Brazil 36, 50, 133
    cashew 36, 37

O

oaks 41
ocelots 6, 77, 112, 114
oil 30, 131, 155
oil bean trees 59
oilbirds 61
oil reserves 153
okapis 101
Olympic Peninsula 40
omnivores 45, 87, 96
Omphalocarpum fruit 95
oncillas 114
orang-utans 94
orchids 12, 16, 33, 49, 56, 57, 133
    Gongora wasp 133
    Rothschild's slipper 57
    Stanhopea hanging-basket 57
Oregon 38, 40
Orinoco River 16, 20, 133, 137, 139, 147, 148, 149
oropendolas 127
otters, giant 143, 144
overfishing 148
overstorey *see under* forests
ovipositors 130, 131
owls 67
oxygen 30, 31, 133, 135, 141, 142, 143, 153, 155

P

pacas 46, 114, 115
Pacific Ocean 3, 20, 38, 40
palms 48, 49, 93
Panama 4, 16, 52, 128
pangolins 65, 118, 119
Pantanal 115
panthers, black 114
Papua New Guinea 18, 53, 64, 79, 104, 119
paradise-kingfishers, white-tailed 46
paradise nut trees 50
parakeets, little star 144
parasites 37, 71, 126, 142
    parasitism 125
parotia, western 78–79
parrots 59, 91, 94, 104, 113
passionflowers 53
peccaries 46, 50, 105, 115
penguins, Megallanic 41
peoples, indigenous 37, 151, 154
perch 93, 143
periwinkles, rosy 37
Peru 16, 63, 84, 104, 131
pheasants 74
Philippines 18, 59, 91, 109, 110
phosphorus 31, 32, 104
photosynthesis 29, 30, 31, 44, 56, 133
pigeons 49, 91, 92, 104

pigmentation 80
pigs 12, 100, 111, 112
   bearded 46, 47, 61
   bush 100
   water pigs 46
pine trees 41
piranha trees 53
piranhas 140, 143
   red-bellied 142
piraracus 143
pitcher plants 132, 134
planarians 57, 106
plant-eaters 100, 109, 131, 141
plants, carnivorous 132
poaching 98
podocarps 41
poisons 102, 104, 107
pollination 4, 28, 49, 50, 53, 57,
   59, 74, 83, 129, 130, 131, 133
pollution 139, 151
Polynesia 20
porcupines, tree 65
possums 66, 103, 110, 111, 113
potassium 31, 32, 84, 104
Prairie Creek Redwoods State
   Park 38
praying mantises 52
predators 108–123
   aerial 110–111
   predatory ants 116–117
   terrestrial 112–115
prehensile tails 64–65
primates 23, 25, 54, 68–71, 75, 86
   see also individual species
proboscises 93, 94
proteins 30, 31, 50, 91, 94, 131
pudús 41
pumas 105, 114
Purús River 139

QR

Queensland 20, 41, 45, 46, 49, 67,
   77, 79, 91, 92, 93, 94, 119, 120,
   127, 147, 150
quinine 36
quolls, spotted-tailed 113, 114
rainfall 4, 26, 27, 28, 32, 37, 38,
   44, 58, 134–135, 136
Rarotonga monarchs 20
Rarotonga starlings 20
rats 12, 46, 87, 91, 111, 132
rattlesnakes 81
rays 147
recycling 34–35, 52, 106, 107, 128
redwoods 38–39
reptiles 46, 65, 66, 114
   see also individual species
resins 83, 87, 123, 133
rhinoceroses 96, 101
rhizomorphs 40
riberry trees 29
Rio de Janeiro 152–153
Rio Negro 133, 140–141, 147
rivers 137, 138–139, 140–141,
   146–147
rodents 6, 81, 100

roots 48, 87, 96
   root systems 32–33, 34,
     48–49, 58
rubber trees 102

S

Sabah 52–53, 58
St Lucia 17
salamanders, web-footed 65
salt 104, 144
San Rafael Falls 17, 18–19
saolas 101
sap-feeders 107, 123, 131
sapanas 106
Sarawak 60, 61
Sarracenia purpurea 132
scorpions 46, 116, 134
screamers, horned 141
seed-eaters 86, 87, 89, 99, 144
seeds 34, 44, 48, 50, 57, 133
   dispersal of 59, 74, 83, 90, 91,
     92, 93, 140
Senegal 17, 69
Sepik River 139
Sequoia National Park 38
Seychelles 132
shad, Laotian 139
sharks 147, 149
sickletails 79
sifakas 23, 29, 45
signalling, animal 72–74, 75, 76
silk cotton trees 58
silver dollars 140
silverfish 116
skates 147
skinks 49, 65
slime moulds 34
sloths 4, 51, 110, 111, 114, 115, 140
smell, sense of 46, 85, 119
snails 87, 99, 106
snakeroot, Indian 37
snakes 6, 12, 46, 61, 92, 111, 134,
   143
   Kapuas mud 81
   tree 67
   vine 134
   see also individual snakes
sodium 34, 84, 104
soil 32, 33, 104
soil-eaters 94, 95, 104, 105
Solomon Islands 20, 65
South Africa 41
South America 3, 4, 5, 6, 16, 17,
   20, 29, 34, 36, 40, 44, 45, 46,
   50, 51, 53, 58, 59, 64, 65, 66,
   72–73, 76, 77, 86, 88, 89, 93,
   103, 104, 105, 107, 110, 114,
   115, 116, 122, 133, 135, 137,
   139, 144, 147, 148, 149, 150,
   153
South China Sea 139
South-east Asia 16, 20, 29, 32,
   35, 36, 37, 54, 56, 57, 58, 65,
   66, 72, 73, 74, 77, 85, 93, 94,
   96, 97, 98, 101, 110, 120,
   122, 139, 153

spices 36
spiders 46, 61, 87, 106, 116,
   120–121, 134, 140, 142
   Agelena 121
   Anelosimus 121
   crab 35
   frog-eating 6
   golden orb-web 120
   huntsman 120
   mahogany-coloured 121
   Theridion 121
squirrels, flying 67, 71
Sri Lanka 35
standardwing, Wallace's 79
Stanhopea 57
starches 28, 30
stems 48, 50, 56, 131
stick insects 49, 53
stilt-houses 140
stingrays 147, 148
storms 31, 32, 44
Strychnopsis thouarsii 23
sugar cane 36, 153
sugar gliders 66, 67
sugars 28, 30, 31, 32, 52, 53, 84,
   93, 131, 133
Sulawesi 20, 24, 29, 99
sulphur 31
Sumatra 87, 94, 96, 102, 113, 129,
   132
sunbirds 84
Sunda Islands 59
superorganisms 116
supplements (to diets) 104–105
Surinam 16
swiftlets 20, 61
Swiss cheese plant 48
symbiosis 125, 126, 128
Symphonia trees 89

T

tadpoles 134, 135, 151
Taiwan 41
talapoins 86, 87
tamanduas 28, 65, 119, 127
tamarins 29, 73, 89
   emperor 88–89
tambaquis 140, 142
tamoatá 141
tapirs 46, 101, 105, 115, 149
tarsiers 25, 29
Tasmania 41
Tasmanian devils 41
teak 36, 37, 153
termites 28, 34, 71, 96, 116, 118,
   119, 123, 126, 127, 128, 132
Tetepare (Solomon Islands) 20
tetras 142, 144
Texas 6
Thailand 113, 147
thrips 59
Tierra del Fuego 41
tigers 46, 112, 113
   Bengal 113, 114
Tijuca National Park 152–153
timber 36–37, 41, 153, 154, 155

titan arum 129
toads, golden 150
tools, use of by primates 69, 71
toucans 65
toxins 151
tree-kangaroos, Lumholtz 103
trees 27, 28, 29, 31, 32, 33, 35, 36,
   37, 38, 41, 50, 52, 53, 58, 59,
   89, 91, 102, 130, 131, 133, 144
   emergents 32, 33, 58, 59, 111
   individually-named (in USA) 38
   largest 38–40, 41
   long-lived 38
   mineral requirements 31
   root systems *see under* roots
   see also individual species
Trinidad 17
Tristan da Cunha 41
tropics 16–23
trumpet trees 131
trunks, tree 32, 94, 95
tucuxi dolphins 143, 144, 147
Turkey 41
turkeys, brush 74
turtles 34, 93, 115, 144
   yellow-spotted river 142

UV

Ubangi River 139
Uganda 93
umbrella trees 131
understorey *see under* forests
USA 40
vampire fish 144
Venezuela 5, 16, 18, 20, 61, 107
venom 106, 121, 147
Vernonia 71
Victoria 41
Vietnam 96, 101, 113, 139
vincristine 37
vines 12, 33, 37, 48, 64, 66, 71, 131
vipers, gaboon 46
volcanoes 24, 25, 32
vultures, black 144

WYZ

Waigeo Island 79
wallabies 111, 114
Wallacea 24
Washington State 38, 40
wasps 116, 126, 127, 130, 131
water gum trees, Francis' 29
water lilies, giant 143, 144
webs, spiders' 120, 121
West Africa 17, 37, 46, 73, 91, 95,
   99, 100, 101, 104, 128
wet season 28–29, 149
whipbird 46
white-eye, rufous-throated 25
worms 34, 47, 57, 96, 106
yams, Mexican 37
Yoshino-Kumano National Park 41
Yukon 114
Zambia 139
zinc 31

PICTURE CREDITS

Abbreviations: T = top; B = bottom; L = left;
R = right

Front cover: Corbis/Jim Zuckerman
Back cover: Corbis/DLILLC

1 naturepl.com/Anup Shah. **2 & 7** FLPA/Frans Lanting. **3** photolibrary.com/Juniors Bildarchiv, TL; ardea.com/Jean Paul Ferrero, ML; Corbis/Michael & Patricia Fogden, MR; naturepl.com/Dietmar Nill, BM. **4** Corbis/Michael & Patricia Fogden, TR; FLPA/Minden Pictures/Mark Moffett, B. **5** Photoshot/Stephen Dalton/NHPA, TL; naturepl.com/Jim Clare, TR; Corbis/Tom Brakefield, ML. **6** naturepl.com/Dietmar Nill, T; FLPA/Minden Pictures/Michael & Patricia Fogden, M; Still Pictures/M. Lane, BL; FLPA/Tom Whittaker, BR. **3–6** Corbis/Carl & Ann Purcell, background. **8–9** thomasmarent.com. **10** photolibrary.com/Olivier Grunewald, TL; naturepl.com/Mary McDonald, TR; FLPA/David Hosking, BL; FLPA/Minden Pictures/Mark Moffett, BR. **11** naturepl.com/David Tipling, TL; Getty Images/Roy Toft, TR; Corbis/Yann Arthus-Bertrand, B. **12–13** left to right: FLPA/Minden Pictures/Michael & Patricia Fogden; photolibrary.com/Mike Powles; FLPA/Jurgen & Christine Sohns; FLPA/Minden Pictures/Frans Lanting; FLPA/Minden Pictures/Michael & Patricia Fogden; FLPA/Frans Lanting; Corbis/Jim Sugar, background. **14–15** photolibrary.com/Olivier Grunewald. **16** FLPA/Larry West. **17** Getty Images/National Geographic Image Collection/Michael K.Nichols, T; FLPA/Frans Lanting, B. **18–19** FLPA/Minden Pictures/Pete Oxford. **20** Corbis/Richard List. **21** FLPA/Minden Pictures/Frans Lanting. **22** naturepl.com/Pete Oxford. **23** photolibrary.com/Mike Powles. **24** naturepl.com/Lucasseck/ARCO. **25** ardea.com/Alan Greensmith, T; naturepl.com/Anup Shah, M. **26–27** Corbis/Eye Ubiquitous/Julia Waterlow. **28** DRK Photo/Michael Fogden. **29** FLPA/Minden Pictures/Michael & Patricia Fogden, T; Robert Harding/Pete Oxford, B. **30–31** South American Pictures/Tony Morrison. **32** ardea.com/Francois Gohier. **33** naturepl.com/Jurgen Freund. **34** FLPA/Minden Pictures/Michael & Patricia Fogden Image Collectionn. **35** naturepl.com/Elio Della Ferrera. **36** Getty Images/National Geographic image Collection/Steve Winter. **37** naturepl.com/Pete Oxford, T; Natural Visions/Heather Angel, B. **38–39** Corbis/Jim Sugar. **40** FLPA/Minden Pictures/Michio Hoshino. **41** Hedgehog House/Rob Brown. **42–43** Corbis/Carl & Ann Purcell. **44** Getty Images/Minden Pictures/Tui De Roy, TL; Hedgehog House/Patricio Robles Gil, TR; Photoshot/NHPA/Stephen Dalton, M; Corbis/Michael & Patricia Fogden, MR. **44–45** Getty Images/Minden Pictures/Norbert Wu, background. **45** Getty Images/National Geographic Image Collection/Steve Winter, TR; naturepl.com/Phil Chapman, ML; FLPA/Neil Bowman, B. **46** naturepl.com/Mary McDonald, T; naturepl.com/Nick Gordon, B. **47** Getty Images/National Geographic Image Collection/Tim Laman. **48** naturepl.com/Dietmar Nill. **49** FLPA/Fritz Polking. **50** Alamy/Douglas Peebles Photography. **51** FLPA/Silvestris Fotoservice. **52** FLPA/Minden Pictures/Mark Moffett, T. **52–53** FLPA/Frans Lanting, B. **53** Corbis/Joe McDonald, B. **54** FLPA/Terry Whittaker, B. **54–55** FLPA/Jurgen & Christine Sohns. **56–57** Auscape International/Davo Blair. **57** DRK Photo/Michael Fogden, L; FLPA/Frans Lanting, R. **58** FLPA/Frans Lanting. **59** naturepl.com/Neil Lucas, L; Science Photo Library/Claude Nuridsany & Marie Perennou, R. **60** FLPA/Mark Newman. **61** Getty Images/National Geographic Image Collection/Steve Winter. **62–63** FLPA/Minden Pictures/Michael & Patricia Fogden. **64** photolibrary.com/Konrad Wothe. **65** Corbis/Kevin Schafer. **66** Photoshot/NHPA/A.N.T. Photo Library. **67** naturepl.com/John

Downer Pr./Tim Macmillan, T; naturepl.com/Solvin Zankl, B. **68–69** FLPA/Peter Davey. **70** naturepl.com/Karen Bass. **71** Getty Images/JH Editorial/ Cyril Ruoso. **72** naturepl.com/David Tipling. **73** photolibrary.com/Philip J DeVries. **74** Corbis/Michael & Patricia Fogden. **75** Corbis/DLILLC. **76** naturepl.com/Phil Savoie. **77** FLPA/Foto Natura/SA Team, L; FLPA/Minden Pictures/Konrad Wothe, BR. **78** FLPA/Minden Pictures/Konrad Wothe. **79** FLPA/Minden Pictures/Michael & Patricia Fogden. **80** Photolibrary.com/Juniors Bildarchiv. **81** Corbis/Papilio/Clive Druett. **82–83** National Geographic Image Collection/Roy Toft. **84–85** naturepl.com/Pete Oxford. **85** Getty Images/National Geographic Image Collection/Roy Toft, B. **86** National Geographic Image Collection/Tim Laman. **87** FLPA/Frans Lanting. **88** photolibrary.com/Martyn Colbeck. **89** ardea.com/A. Greensmith. **90** Getty Images/National Geographic Image Collection/Tim Laman. **91** National Geographic Image Collection/Tim Laman. **92** DRK Photo/Martin Harvey. **93** National Geographic Image Collection/Tim Laman. **94** FLPA/Minden Pictures/Konrad Wothe. **95** Alamy/Arco Images/P. Weimann. **96** photolibrary.com/Mary Plage. **96–97** Science Photo Library/Art Wolfe. **98** FLPA/Gerard Lacz. **99** FLPA/Terry Whittaker. **100–101** Corbis/Theo Allofs. **100** ardea.com/Nick Gordon, T. **101** naturepl.com/Bruce Davidson, T. **102** Getty Images/National Geographic Image Collection/Tim Laman, L; FLPA/Foto Natura/Flip de Nooyer, R. **103** DRK Photo/Martin Harvey. **104** FLPA/Minden Pictures/Frans Lanting. **105** photolibrary.com/Martyn Colbeck. **106** DRK Photo/Denise Tackett, TL. **106** DRK Photo/Denise Tackett, T. **107** DRK Photo/Martin Harvey, T. **108–109** Still Pictures/Gunter Ziesler. **110** ardea.com/Kenneth W. Fink. **111** FLPA/David Hosking. **112** Getty Images/National Geographic Image Collection/Ed George. **113** naturepl.com/Dave Watts. **114** FLPA/Minden Pictures/Frans Lanting. **115** ardea.com/Nick Gordon. **116** naturepl.com/Martin Dohrn. **118** FLPA/Frans Lantin. **119** DRK Photo/Martin Harvey. **120** National Georgraphic Image Collection/Tim Laman. **121** National Geographic Image Collection/Darlyne A. Murawski. **122** naturepl.com/Nick Garbutt. **123** ardea.com/Nick Gordon. **124–125** FLPA/Minden Pictures/Mark Moffett. **126** Photoshot/A.N.T./Cliff & Dawn Frith. **127** naturepl.com/Kim Taylor. **128** Alamy/Edward Parker. **129** naturepl.com/Neil Lucas. **130** FLPA/Minden Pictures/Michael & Patricia Fogden. **131** FLPA/Minden Pictures/Mark Moffett. **132** Dennis J. Merbach. **133** Science Photo Library/Dr Morley Read. **134–135** FLPA/Minden Pictures/Mark Moffett. **136–137** FLPA/Frans Lanting. **138–139** Corbis/Yann Arthus-Bertrand. **140–141** South American Pictures/Tony Morrison. **141** FLPA/Frank W. Lane. **142** photolibrary.com/OSF/Michael Fogden. **143** ardea.com/M. Watson. **144** naturepl.com/John Downer Pr./Tim Macmillan. **145** FLPA/Frans Lanting. **146–147** Getty Images/National Geographic Image Collection/Joel Sartore. **148–149** Corbis/Joe McDonald. **149** Onasia.com/Suthep Kritsanavarin. **150–151** FLPA/Minden Pictures/Gerry Ellis. **151** FLPA/Minden Pictures/Michael & Patricia Fogden. **152–153** FLPA/Frans Lanting. **154** Photoshot/Woodfall Wild Images/Tony Martin. **155** Still Pictures/Peter Arnold/Luiz C. Marigo.

Artworks:
Bradbury & Williams: 27, 40–41, 98
GeoInovations: 16
Glyn Walton: 30

NATURE'S MIGHTY POWERS: RAIN FORESTS
was published by The Reader's Digest Association Ltd, London. It was created and produced for Reader's Digest by Toucan Books Ltd, London.

The Reader's Digest Association Ltd,
11 Westferry Circus,
Canary Wharf,
London E14 4HE
www.readersdigest.co.uk

First edition copyright © 2008

Written by
Michael Bright

FOR TOUCAN BOOKS
Editors Jane Chapman, Helen Douglas-Cooper, Andrew Kerr-Jarrett
Designers Bradbury & Williams
Picture researchers Wendy Brown, Sharon Southren, Christine Vincent
Proofreader Marion Dent
Indexer Michael Dent

FOR READER'S DIGEST
Project editor Christine Noble
Art editor Julie Bennett
Pre-press account manager Dean Russell
Product production manager Claudette Bramble
Production controller Katherine Bunn

READER'S DIGEST, GENERAL BOOKS
Editorial director Julian Browne
Art director Anne-Marie Bulat

Colour origination Colour Systems Ltd, London
Printed and bound in China

We are committed to both the quality of our products and the service we provide to our customers. We value your comments, so please feel free to contact us on 08705 113366 or via our website at **www.readersdigest.co.uk**

If you have any comments or suggestions about the content of our books, you can email us at **gbeditorial@readersdigest.co.uk**

CONCEPT CODE: UK0138/G/S
BOOK CODE: 636-008 UP0000-1
ISBN: 978-0-276-44296-4
ORACLE CODE: 356500013H.00.24